A Nation's Heritage

*A Town-by-Town Guide to Colonial and
Revolutionary War History in the South*

Max Victor Alper

Globe
Pequot

Essex, Connecticut

Globe
Pequot

An imprint of The Globe Pequot Publishing Group, Inc.
64 South Main Street
Essex, CT 06426
www.globepequot.com

British Library Cataloguing in Publication Information available

Library of Congress Cataloging-in-Publication Data available

9781493094530 (paperback)
9781493094554 (electronic)

For Joey McGill

CONTENTS

CONTENTS

Acknowledgments

I AM GRATEFUL FOR THE COURTEOUS ASSISTANCE OF THE STAFFS OF THE New York Public Library, Charleston County Library, Wilmington Public Library, Charlottesville Public Library, and the libraries of the University of South Carolina and the University of Virginia. The following institutions also have been most helpful: Charleston Museum, Georgetown Chamber of Commerce, Hillsborough Chamber of Commerce, Bern Historical Society, Edenton Historical Commission, North Carolina Department of Archives, Virginia State Travel Service, Virginia Museum of History and Culture, Monticello Area Historical Society, Alamance Battleground State Historic Site, Guilford Courthouse National Military Park, Yorktown Battlefield Site, North Carolina Museum of History, the United States National Park Service.

I am indebted to the Library of Congress and to the National Archives for their assistance and access to their extraordinary resources. In addition, I wish to thank the National Portrait Gallery and the National Museum of American History—both of the Smithsonian Institution—for their cooperation. They are all guardians of our nation's historical treasures.

Special thanks to the following individuals: Hope Biddle for assistance updating historic site entrance information; Joey McGill for many kindnesses and for creating conditions conducive for research and comfort; Christina and John Dickhoff for their emotional support throughout the years; and Mark Fehrs Haukohl for insights into art and history.

To the Reader

This book describes major events and battles of the American Revolution and presents practical information for travelers. Although Colonial and Revolutionary War sites are emphasized in the text, subordinate sections—"Non-Revolutionary Sites of Interest" and "Recommended Side Trips"—are included to permit travelers to experience other aspects of a region's history. The suggested Walking and Driving Tours list the individual sites in the order encountered by sightseers. Afterward, these sites (arranged *alphabetically* according to category) are described in detail.

The narrative, which begins with the British siege of Charleston and ends with the death of George Washington at Mount Vernon, takes the reader on a northward journey—from South Carolina into North Carolina and then Virginia. Since the narrative units are self-contained, however, one may start at any point.

Visitors to sites are advised to verify schedules and admission fees, which are subject to change. During America's 250th Anniversary celebration, historic sites—especially those administered by the US Park Service—will modify hours and fees. Because many historic houses are being restored, their contents may differ slightly from the descriptions herein. If recommended roads are under construction, alternate routes may be followed with the aid of a GPS navigation system. Every effort has been made to print the most recent data, but the author and the publisher cannot be responsible for any changes of information or omissions.

As you read these pages, it is hoped that the fascinating drama of the American Revolution may excite your imagination and stir your spirit.

Chronology of the American Revolution

1770	
MARCH 5	The Boston Massacre: British soldiers fire on a crowd in Boston, resulting in the deaths of five persons.
APRIL 12	Parliament repeals duties (imposed by the Townshend Revenue Act, November 20, 1767) on paper, glass, lead, and dyestuff but retains the tax on tea.
1771	
MAY 16	Royal Governor Tryon's forces crush a Regulator uprising at Alamance, North Carolina.
JUNE 19	Six Regulators are executed at Hillsborough, North Carolina.
1772	
JUNE 9	Rhode Islanders attack and burn the British ship *Gaspee*.
NOVEMBER 2	Samuel Adams organizes the first Committee of Correspondence in Boston.
1773	
MAY 10	To save the mismanaged East India Company from bankruptcy, Parliament partially refunds taxes the company had paid and permits shipment of tea directly to retailers in the American colonies. Established importers and citizens protest.

DECEMBER 16	Boston Tea Party: Men disguised as Indians board three ships in Boston Harbor and heave 342 chests of tea into the water.
1774	
MAY–JUNE	The Coercive Acts ("Intolerable Acts") passed by Parliament go into effect. The Massachusetts Government Act (May 20) modifies the provincial government by providing a new council under a military governor, who also has authority over town meetings. The Administration of Justice Act (May 20) protects officials of the Crown accused of capital offenses by permitting them to be tried elsewhere. The Boston Port Bill (June 1) closes Boston to commerce. The extension of the Quartering Act (June 2) provides for the housing of British troops in America.
JUNE 22	The Quebec Act grants the territory between the Ohio and Mississippi Rivers to the province of Quebec, thereby establishing Roman Catholicism and French civil law in the area.
SEPTEMBER 5	The First Continental Congress (fifty-six delegates from twelve colonies) meets in Philadelphia.
SEPTEMBER 9	Delegates from towns in Suffolk County, Massachusetts, adopt the Suffolk Resolves, which denounce the Coercive Acts as unconstitutional and recommend economic sanctions against England.
OCTOBER 25	Angry women of Edenton, North Carolina, sign a resolution protesting the tax on tea and the harsh policies of the British government.
1775	
MARCH 23	Patrick Henry delivers his "Give me Liberty or give me Death" speech in Richmond, Virginia.
APRIL 19	At Lexington, Massachusetts, British soldiers fire on the Patriots and then march to Concord, where the Redcoats are forced to retreat.

APRIL 19	The siege of Boston begins: Patriot forces surround the British garrisoned in the city.
APRIL 20	Royal Governor Dunmore of Virginia orders powder and munitions secretly removed from the Williamsburg Magazine, causing Patriots to march on the town.
MAY 10	The Second Continental Congress convenes in Philadelphia.
MAY 10	Fort Ticonderoga, New York, is captured by a detachment of Green Mountain Boys under Ethan Allen and troops commanded by Benedict Arnold.
MAY 24	John Hancock is elected president of the Continental Congress.
JUNE 11–12	The first naval battle of the American Revolution occurs near Machias, Maine, resulting in the capture of two British ships: the *Margaretta* and the *Unity.*
JUNE 15	The Second Continental Congress elects George Washington as Commander in Chief of the Continental Army.
JUNE 17	At the Battle of Bunker Hill (Breed's Hill), the British rout the Patriots but sustain high casualties.
JULY 3	In Cambridge, Massachusetts, Washington assumes command of the army.
DECEMBER 22	Esek Hopkins is appointed Commander in Chief of the Continental Navy.
1776	
JANUARY 1	The American assault on Quebec fails.
JANUARY 9	Thomas Paine publishes *Common Sense*, urging Americans to declare their independence from Great Britain.
FEBRUARY 27	The Patriots are victorious at the Battle of Moores Creek, North Carolina.
MARCH 17	The British evacuate Boston.

APRIL 17	John Barry is the first commissioned officer of the Continental Navy to capture a British warship, the *Edward.*
JUNE 28	Patriot forces on Sullivan's Island, South Carolina, repulse the British fleet, preventing its entry into Charleston Harbor.
JULY 4	The Continental Congress adopts the Declaration of Independence.
AUGUST 27	The British overpower the Americans during the Battle of Long Island.
AUGUST 29	Washington's defeated troops retreat to Manhattan.
SEPTEMBER 15	British warships move into the East River and force the Americans to withdraw from mid-Manhattan.
SEPTEMBER 16	At Harlem Heights, New York, the Americans prove their ability to drive back the enemy.
SEPTEMBER 21	Nathan Hale is captured.
SEPTEMBER 26	Congress appoints Benjamin Franklin a commissioner to Paris.
OCTOBER 28	The Patriots are defeated at White Plains, New York.
NOVEMBER 16	Fort Washington on Manhattan is captured by British and German troops.
NOVEMBER 20	Americans abandon Fort Lee, New Jersey.
DECEMBER 8	The British occupy Newport, Rhode Island.
DECEMBER 26	After crossing the Delaware River, Washington and his men surprise the Hessians quartered at Trenton.
1777	
JANUARY 3	At the Battle of Princeton, Washington's counteroffensive compels the British to withdraw.
JANUARY 6	Washington establishes his winter headquarters at Morristown, New Jersey.

JUNE 13	The Marquis de Lafayette arrives in America to join the Patriot cause.
JUNE 14	The Continental Congress passes a resolution authorizing the design of the American flag.
AUGUST 16	Americans overpower their enemy during the Battle of Bennington.
SEPTEMBER 11	General William Howe's troops defeat Washington's army at the Battle of Brandywine, Pennsylvania.
SEPTEMBER 18	The Continental Congress flees Philadelphia.
SEPTEMBER 19	Patriots clash with General John Burgoyne's soldiers at Freeman's Farm (Saratoga Campaign).
SEPTEMBER 20	General Anthony Wayne's men are caught in a surprise attack, the "Paoli Massacre."
SEPTEMBER 26	General Howe occupies Philadelphia.
OCTOBER 4	American strategy fails at the Battle of Germantown.
OCTOBER 7	Americans defeat Burgoyne's troops at Bemis Heights (Saratoga Campaign).
OCTOBER 17	General Burgoyne surrenders his army at Saratoga—a serious defeat for the British.
NOVEMBER 15	Congress adopts the Articles of Confederation.
NOVEMBER 16	Fort Mifflin, Pennsylvania, is abandoned by the Patriots.
DECEMBER 19	The Continental Army establishes its camp at Valley Forge (until June 18–19, 1778).
1778	
FEBRUARY 6	France signs a Treaty of Alliance with America.
MAY 18	General Howe turns over command of British forces in America to Henry Clinton.
JUNE 18	Clinton evacuates Philadelphia and marches toward New York City.
JUNE 28	A series of confused assaults occurs at Monmouth, New Jersey.

JULY 3–5	Indians and Loyalists destroy houses and massacre residents of Wyoming Valley, Pennsylvania.
DECEMBER 29	The British capture Savannah, Georgia.
1779	
JUNE 16	Spain declares war on Great Britain.
JULY 5	New Haven, Connecticut, is attacked by a British expedition.
JULY 16	General Anthony Wayne's men capture the British-held fortification at Stony Point, New York.
SEPTEMBER 23	In an important naval battle, John Paul Jones forces the surrender of the British ship *Serapis*.
SEPTEMBER 27	John Jay is named minister to Spain.
OCTOBER 9	A Franco-American attempt to retake Savannah fails.
OCTOBER 25	The British evacuate Newport, Rhode Island.
1780	
MARCH 15	Congress devalues American currency.
MAY 12	Charleston, South Carolina, is occupied by the British.
JULY 10	French troops under Rochambeau arrive at Newport.
AUGUST 16	Americans suffer a serious defeat at Camden, South Carolina.
SEPTEMBER 23	Benedict Arnold's treachery is discovered.
OCTOBER 2	Major John André, a British spy who negotiated with Arnold for the betrayal of West Point, is executed.
OCTOBER 7	Patriot forces crush their adversary at Kings Mountain, South Carolina.
OCTOBER 14	General Nathanael Greene assumes command of the American forces in the South.

1781	
JANUARY 5–7	British forces plunder Richmond, Virginia.
JANUARY 17	The Patriots are victorious at Cowpens, South Carolina.
FEBRUARY 20	Henry ("Light-Horse Harry") Lee routs a detachment of Loyalists marching to join the army of Cornwallis at Hillsborough, North Carolina.
FEBRUARY 20	Congress appoints Robert Morris superintendent of finance.
MARCH 1	The last state formally ratifies the Articles of Confederation.
MARCH 15	Cornwallis wins the Battle of Guilford Courthouse, North Carolina, but approximately a quarter of his soldiers are casualties.
APRIL 23	Americans capture Fort Watson, South Carolina.
APRIL 25	The Americans are defeated at Hobkirk's Hill, South Carolina.
JULY 6	Cornwallis repulses Lafayette near Jamestown, Virginia.
AUGUST 22	Cornwallis garrisons his troops at Yorktown, Virginia.
SEPTEMBER 5	In a naval engagement off Virginia, the French fleet inflicts heavy damage on British vessels.
SEPTEMBER 8	At Eutaw Springs, South Carolina, the British take control of the battlefield after Patriot troops are thrown into disorder.
SEPTEMBER 28	The American and French siege of Yorktown begins.
OCTOBER 19	Cornwallis surrenders his army at Yorktown.
1782	
MARCH 20	England's prime minister, Lord North, resigns.
NOVEMBER 30	American and English commissioners sign the Preliminary Articles of Peace.
DECEMBER 14	British troops evacuate Charleston.

1783	
JUNE 24	Congress flees Philadelphia after troops in the city revolt.
SEPTEMBER 3	The Treaty of Paris officially ending the war and acknowledging America's independence is signed.
NOVEMBER 25	The British evacuate New York City.
DECEMBER 23	Washington resigns his commission as commander in chief of the Continental Army and returns to Mount Vernon.

SOUTH CAROLINA

Charleston

REVOLUTIONARY WAR HISTORY

In 1779, British war strategists decided to attempt to capture the Southern colonies through a campaign beginning in South Carolina and moving into Virginia. Sir Henry Clinton, Commander in Chief of the British forces in America, decided to first establish a base at Charleston (Charles Town) and then advance northward to rally the numerous Loyalists to support and join his military operations. (A previous effort in 1776 had been repulsed when the British fleet was unable to pass the guns of the fort on Sullivan's Island at the entrance to Charleston Harbor.)

The siege of Charleston began in late March 1780. On the upper end of Charleston Neck, the British constructed three sets of parallel entrenchments connected to one another by a series of transecting trenches. Batteries were erected at strategic positions. From the opposite side of the city, at the entrance to Charleston Harbor, eight warships under the command of Admiral Mariot Arbuthnot loomed menacingly.

The defense of the city was entrusted to General Benjamin Lincoln, who commanded a woefully inadequate force of 5,600 men against the adversary's well-trained 14,000 troops. Undaunted, he ordered the building of a small canal to repel a foot attack and issued instructions for the construction of several breastworks and redoubts. Across the mouth of the Cooper River, a log-and-chain boom was extended as a buffer for the already blockaded American ships.

But these maneuvers were in vain. After a summons to surrender was rejected by General Lincoln on April 10, the British assault commenced. On April 13, the batteries rained red-hot shells and fireballs on Charleston, which set countless buildings aflame. As the bombardment

Harbor Scene—English Ship Firing a Gun (detail) by Peter Monomy (METROPOLITAN MUSEUM OF ART; GIFT OF WILLIAM P. CLYDE)

continued, word came that the northern defense at Moncks Corner had fallen to the British and cut off escape routes due to the military leadership of Colonel Banastre Tarleton. When Clinton's troops approached nearer to the city, Governor Rutledge and three members of the City Council fled.

On May 6, Fort Moultrie surrendered to the British fleet without firing a shot. The merciless assault of 200 artillery pieces on May 9 finally broke the spirit of the townspeople. Three days later, the American troops laid down their arms. The soldiers became prisoners of war, and the militia and armed residents were released on their promise not to bear arms again.

Losses were light—76 men killed and 189 injured on the British side; 89 men killed and 138 wounded on the American side. The surrender of Charleston resulted in the loss of the Southern Continental Army, including 311 cannon and thousands of muskets.

The British occupied the city until December 14, 1782.

VISITOR INFORMATION

Information, pamphlets, and books are available at the **Charleston Visitor Center**, 375 Meeting Street; (800) 774-0006.

Charleston Metro Chamber of Commerce, 4922 O'Hear Avenue, Suite 101; (843) 577-251C

GUIDED TOURS

Palmetto Tours, (843) 367-5462
Charleston 101, (843) 556-4753
Charleston Guide Service, (843) 814-7900
Grayline Charleston, (843) 722-4444

PUBLIC TRANSPORTATION Charleston Area Regional Transportation Authority, 3664 Leads Avenue; call (843) 323-4734 or visit www.ridecarta.com for bus routes and schedules.

TAXI SERVICE Charleston Bike Taxi, (843) 532-8663; Charleston Black Cab Company, (843) 216-2627

WALKING TOURS Most of Charleston's major points of interest can be seen in three walking tours. The listing below consists primarily of Revolutionary War sites. ("NR" signifies an important non-Revolutionary site; "P" indicates a historic Colonial house that is now a private residence.)

Tour A

Area bounded by Cumberland Street on the north, Tradd Street on the south, East Bay Street on the east, and Meeting Street on the west.

Start at East Bay and Broad Streets.

Exchange Building

Old Slave Market (NR)

Pink House

Huguenot Church (NR)

Dock Street Theater

St. Philip's Church

Powder Magazine
Market Hall (NR)
Gibbes Art Museum (NR)
City Hall (NR)
Washington Square
St. Michael's Church
Cabbage Row (NR)
Heyward-Washington House
Bee House (P)
End at Tradd and Church Streets.

Tour B

Area bounded by Tradd Street on the north, South Battery on the south, East Bay Street on the east, and Meeting Street on the west.
Start at Tradd and Meeting Streets.
Nathaniel Russell House (NR)
Royal Governor's Residence (P)
William Washington House (P)
Gibbes House (P)
White Point Gardens
Rainbow Row
End at Tradd and East Bay Streets.

Tour C

Area bounded by Broad Street on the north, Lamboll Street on the south, King Street on the east, and Legare Street on the west.
Start at Broad and King Streets.
Ramsay House (P)
Izard House (P)
Rutledge House (P)
British Staff Quarters (P)
Brewton House (P)
End at King and Ladson Streets.

COLONIAL AND REVOLUTIONARY WAR SITES
DOCK STREET THEATER

135 Church Street. Box office open Tuesday through Friday, 1 p.m. to 5 p.m.: Saturday, 1 p.m. to 5 p.m. during performances. Phone: (843) 577-5967. The Dock Street Theater—the first building in America designed exclusively for theatrical productions—opened on February 12, 1736, with George Farquhar's well-known comedy *The Recruiting Officer* (1706). Fire destroyed the structure in 1740, and a new theater was built on the site in 1754. Townspeople thronged to the opening night to see Nicholas Rowe's *The Fair Penitent* (1703). The well-known acting companies of Lewis Hallam and David Douglass frequently appeared at the Dock Street Theater.

Charlestonians so enjoyed dramatic productions that in 1773 a larger building had to be constructed on the site to accommodate the theater-going crowds. One historian observed that the theater's first season was "the most brilliant of Colonial America." That year 118 productions were staged, including comedies, Shakespearean tragedies, and operas.

Few performances were given during the Revolutionary War. The building on Dock Street (present-day Queen Street) escaped destruction during the British bombardment and occupation. After the war, the theater was closed because public officials considered the performances too frivolous. By 1791, all legal strictures were removed and entertainment was again permitted here in time for George Washington's visit to Charleston.

Dock Street Theater, Charleston (LIBRARY OF CONGRESS, PRINTS AND PHOTOGRAPHS DIVISION)

In the early 1800s, the Planter's Hotel, which offered lavish accommodations for planters and travelers, was built on this site, and it included an auditorium. According to tradition, actor Junius Brutus Booth (father of Edwin Booth), who occupied a room here in 1838, became so enraged during an argument with his manager that he tried to kill him with a hotel andiron!

By the late nineteenth century, the building had deteriorated to a pale shadow of its former elegance. In the early 1930s, the federal government granted funds for a project to restore the Planter's Hotel and to create a reconstruction of the Dock Street Theater.

The present building, which opened on November 26, 1937, is noted for its fine Adam-style woodwork in the hotel rooms and its faithfully reproduced interior of a Georgian playhouse. (Today, the theater is operated by Charleston Stage, the resident acting company.) The restored facade is graced by a delicate cast-iron balcony that was part of the original building.

ELFE HOUSE

54 Queen Street. Not open to the public. This was the home of Thomas Elfe (1719–1775), one of Charleston's most important cabinetmakers, who came to the colony from England in 1747 and built this house thirteen years later. All the original cypress paneling has been preserved in this four-room structure, and reproductions of Elfe's furniture are on display. The small building in the rear was a workshop.

Elfe's furniture was highly prized by residents of the area, and his account books reflect a profitable enterprise.

EXCHANGE BUILDING AND PROVOST DUNGEON

122 East Bay Street. Open Monday through Saturday, 9 a.m. to 5 p.m.; Sunday, 11 a.m. to 5 p.m. Adults $16, children (under 6) free, youth (7–12) $12. Phone: (843) 727-2165. Before the present building was constructed, a guardhouse—standing behind the protective walls of the Half Moon Battery—was located on this site, which then fronted on the water. Completed about 1704, the two-story structure served as the military center of Charleston.

It was here that the notorious pirate Stede Bonnet and his crew were confined prior to their execution in 1718. Stede, an educated man of good family and a retired British army major, had joined Edward Teach ("Blackbeard") in his raids on South Carolina coastal towns. In June 1718, the pirate fleet captured nine vessels, one of which carried Samuel Wragg, a member of the Grand Council, who was held for ransom. When the pirates' demands were met, Wragg and the other captives were freed, but the citizens of Charleston had become outraged. They empowered Colonel William Rhett, commanding two sloops and 160 men, to track down the buccaneers. A month later, Rhett captured Bonnet and his crew off the North Carolina coast and returned to Charleston in triumph.

In 1771, the guardhouse was replaced by the present building, which was designed by a local architect, William Rigby Naylor, and built by John and Peter Horlbeck. The structure, which cost £44,000, was financed by a duty on rum, wine, bread, and biscuits.

In 1773, Charlestonians rebelled against the British tax on tea by interfering with the unloading of ship cargoes. Hundreds of chests of East India tea were seized from Captain Carling's ship on December 22,

Exchange Building, Charleston (LIBRARY OF CONGRESS, PRINTS AND PHOTOGRAPHS DIVISION)

1773, and placed in the underground chambers of the Exchange Building. Several shipments seized from other vessels were stored here as well.

Representatives from all parts of South Carolina assembled in the Exchange Building in 1774 to elect delegates to the First Continental Congress. Christopher Gadsden, Henry Middleton, John Rutledge, Thomas Lynch Jr., and Edward Rutledge were chosen for the assembly that would decide the issue of independence from England. (Middleton served as the second president of the Congress from October 22, 1774, to May 10, 1775.)

On November 15, 1774, Charleston had its own "Tea Party." After Captain Samuel Ball had refused an ultimatum to return to England or destroy his tea, several merchants came aboard and dumped the tea into the harbor. A crowd of spectators gathered near this site.

In March 1776, the South Carolina Provincial Congress met here to establish the first independent government in America. John Rutledge was chosen president and Henry Laurens vice president.

When the British occupied Charleston in 1780, they chose the Exchange Building for their military headquarters. From the steps of this building, Lord William Campbell, the newly appointed royal governor, heard his commission read to him, but the hostility of the local citizenry was embarrassingly obvious—only fifteen persons attended the ceremonies. In view of the incendiary political situation, the usual rounds of cannon fire that accompanied such events were dispensed with.

Several days before the British captured Charleston, General William Moultrie (who, commanding the fort on Sullivan's Island, had defeated the British forces in June 1776) and his comrades carried 10,000 pounds of powder from the magazine to the Exchange cellar. It remained there—hidden behind a bricked-up wall—until the city was returned to Patriot control. Throughout the occupation, the British were sitting on a virtual powder keg without knowing it!

The cellar of the Exchange Building was converted into a prison—the Provost Dungeon—where outspoken Patriot men and women were shackled. Political activists from all parts of South Carolina were driven in chains in a forced march to Charleston and incarcerated here.

Crowded together in the dark, vermin-infested dungeon, many of the weakened prisoners fell prey to "jail fever" and died.

After the Revolutionary War, the Exchange Building was the scene of many festive events, such as the celebration honoring President George Washington in May 1791. To the president's delight, the ladies gave him an unusual welcome. Many women wore sashes across their bosoms with the words "Long Life to the President." Others, hoping to flatter their distinguished guest when he greeted them with a hand kiss, commissioned local artists to paint Washington's image on the back of their hands.

In 1818, the Exchange Building was sold to the federal government for use as a custom house. At the end of the century, it served as a post office. It was later deeded to the South Carolina Society of the Daughters of the American Revolution.

HEYWARD-WASHINGTON HOUSE

87 Church Street. Open Monday through Saturday, 10 a.m. to 5 p.m.; Sunday, 12 p.m. to 5 p.m. Adults $15, children (under 2) free, children (3–12) $6, youth (13–17) $12. Phone: (843) 722-2996. Daniel Heyward, a wealthy rice planter from St. Luke's Parish, built this house in 1770. After his death, it passed to his son Thomas, who was a member of the South Carolina House of Commons (1772); served on the Committee of Safety (1775); and, as a delegate to the Continental Congress (1776), signed the Declaration of Independence.

A captain of artillery, he took part in the defense of Savannah (1779) and the siege of Charleston (1780). After the British captured Charleston, Heyward was sent, along with around sixty other prominent Charlestonians, to be incarcerated at Fort San Marcos in St. Augustine, Florida (then under British control). According to legend, on July 4, 1781—the fifth anniversary of the adoption of the Declaration—these political prisoners determined to demonstrate their patriotism. Heyward is credited with writing a rousing ballad that was sung by his compatriots until their British guards silenced them.

During Thomas Heyward's imprisonment, his wife and her sister, Mrs. George Abbott Hall, continued to occupy this house. When, on

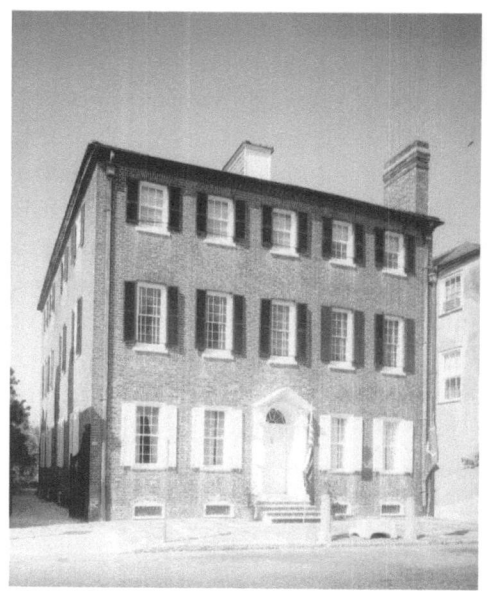

Heyward-Washington House, Charleston

the evening of May 12, 1781, the British ordered Charleston residents to commemorate the first anniversary of the fall of their city by placing lighted candles in their windows, Mrs. Heyward boldly disobeyed. Enraged by this act of defiance, Loyalists mobbed the house, and during the melee Mrs. Hall suffered a stroke and died. Mrs. Heyward spent her final days in exile in Philadelphia.

During George Washington's visit to Charleston in May 1791—while still serving as president of the United States—he lodged in the Heyward house. As Thomas Heyward was then residing at his plantation, White Hall (in St. Luke's Parish), the City Council rented his fine Georgian mansion for a week and installed a housekeeper and servants to care for the distinguished visitor. Washington arrived on May 2 at Haddrell's Point (on the north side of the Cooper River opposite Charleston), where he was met by a delegation of prominent citizens, including John Bee Holmes (the city recorder), Charles Cotesworth Pinckney (a former representative to the Constitutional Convention), and Edward Rutledge (a former delegate to the Continental Congress). The president was then rowed across the river in a flat-bottom boat, accompanied by scores of small crafts filled with cheering citizens.

Washington was welcomed at Prioleau's Wharf (at the end of Queen Street) by Governor Charles Pinckney, Lieutenant-Governor Isaac Holmes, and members of the City Council. The president was then conducted to the Exchange Building, where he reviewed a parade. That evening he attended a state dinner at the governor's residence. During the remainder of the week, he was feted by prominent Charlestonians, made official visits to the city's sites, and was honored at a ball at the Exchange Building. He also received visitors at the Heyward house.

The furnishings of the Heyward-Washington House are truly elegant. In the **Reception Room,** to the right of the entrance hallway, stands an impressive library case. Made in Charleston (possibly at the shop of cabinetmaker Robert Walker), this piece is monumental in proportions. A hole in the upper section of the right side was made by a small shell in 1865, when federal troops occupied the city.

Above the mid-eighteenth-century slant-top desk, of kingwood imported from Brazil, hangs a portrait of George Washington painted on the reverse side of the glass. It is a copy after Gilbert Stuart.

To the left of the fireplace is a case containing memorabilia of the Heyward family. Among the cherished items is a sash worn by Eliza Lucas Pinckney at the Charleston reception for the first president. Washington and Mrs. Pinckney had become such close friends that when she died, he asked to be one of her pallbearers.

Like guardian spirits, Daniel Heyward (builder of this house) and his first wife, Mary Miles—austerely portrayed in the Stolle portraits (after Theus)—look down at the **Dining Room** furnishings: the Chippendale-style chairs clustered around the dining room table; the "cellarette," a container for chilling wines; the Crown Derby dinner set; and the Vieux Paris porcelain dessert service once owned by Thomas Heyward Jr.

During his visit, Washington occupied the second-floor **Bedroom** to the right of the stairway. The Charleston-made four-poster bed here belonged to the Heyward family. The fine bow-front chest of drawers is distinguished by fluted quarter-columns on the corners and ogee bracket feet. Nearby stands a corner chair with removable seat, becoming a convenience or "pot chair." The Hepplewhite-design washstand, decorated with eagles and thirteen stars, is highly treasured because it is said to have been used by Washington when he resided in Philadelphia as president.

The handsome **Drawing Room**, which is fully paneled, contains delicate fretwork mantel trim, two beautifully carved doors mounted by broken pediments, and decorative ceiling molding. In the center of the room stands a tea table in the Chinese Chippendale style and two chairs attributed to Thomas Elfe, the famous Charleston cabinetmaker.

On the fine marble-top table (c. 1760)—below the round English Chippendale mirror—rests a mahogany clock made by John James Himley, a Huguenot clockmaker who worked in Charleston near the end of the eighteenth century. (The misspelling of "Charleston" makes this a curiosity piece.)

A marble bust of George Washington on the slant-top desk once belonged to the family of Colonel William Washington, the president's cousin.

Among the furnishings in the blue-and-white **Withdrawing Room** is a mahogany library case with a broken-arch top, bracket feet, and elaborate satinwood-and-ivory inlay. Considered one of the finest cases of its kind made in America, it was owned by John Bee Holmes, recorder of Charleston. Holmes's portrait, hanging nearby, was painted by Samuel F. B. Morse (1791–1872), famed for his invention of the telegraph, who lived in Charleston for several years while working as a portraitist.

The ceramic figure on the mantel is a representation of Benjamin Franklin, even though it is mislabeled "Washington" on the base. Above the mantel is a portrait (after Jeremiah Theus) of Thomas Heyward Jr.

MARION SQUARE

Calhoun Street between King and Meeting Streets. This public park was named for General Francis Marion (1732–1795, born near Georgetown, South Carolina), who became known as the "Swamp Fox" because of his ability to elude the British by escaping to safety through the swamps.

On the west side of the square stands the only remaining section of the Tabby Horn Work—the fortification walls of the Colonial defense system that extended across the city from river to river.

Dominating the square is a statue of John C. Calhoun (1782–1850), a South Carolina statesman who served as secretary of war (1817–1825), vice president (1825–1832) under John Quincy Adams, senator (1833–1844), and secretary of state (1844–1845).

POWDER MAGAZINE

79 Cumberland Street. Open daily, 10 a.m. to 4 p.m. For tours, call for appointment. Phone: (843) 722-9350. Built in 1713, the Powder Magazine was originally part of the Carteret Bastion, which protected the northwest corner of Colonial Charleston. The squat, eight-gabled structure, with walls thirty-two inches thick, has groined vaulting of brick and tabby (a mortar made from oyster shells). The colony's gunpowder supply was stored in this building.

On display in the museum are several eighteenth-century brocade dresses—one of them from the family of Eliza Lucas Pinckney, who introduced the indigo plant into South Carolina. One can also see clothes worn by Charlestonian Henry Laurens (1724–1792), president of the Continental Congress (1777–1778), who was taken prisoner by the British; transported to England, where he was incarcerated in the Tower of London; and later returned in a prisoner exchange (1782) for General Charles Cornwallis.

Engravings of South Carolina's four signers of the Declaration of Independence—Edward Rutledge, Arthur Middleton, Thomas Lynch Jr., and Thomas Heyward Jr.—hang on the austere brick walls. Nearby cases contain dainty Rockingham cups and saucers, handsome jewel boxes brought to Charleston by French Huguenots, ornate Dresden candlestick holders, and fine pieces of Staffordshire china (owned by Robert Marion, nephew of Francis Marion, the "Swamp Fox").

The two cannon in front of the Powder Magazine, which bear the seal of King George III, were originally placed along the waterfront.

ST. MICHAEL'S CHURCH

71 Broad Street. Office open Monday through Thursday, 8:30 a.m. to 4:30 p.m.; Friday, 8:30 a.m. to 12:30 p.m. Church and Courtyard open Monday through Thursday, 9 a.m. to 4 p.m. Sunday services at 8, 9, and 11 a.m. Phone: (843) 723-0603. St. Michael's was completed in 1762, and the building remains unchanged except for the addition of a sacristy (in 1883). Designed by local architect Samuel Cardy, the church has a Doric portico and a 190-foot segmented steeple. In Colonial times, as a fire-warning device, a lighted lantern was hung from the spire on a long pole pointing in the direction of the conflagration.

During the Revolutionary War, Major P. Traille of the Royal Artillery took down St. Michael's bells and sent them to England as a prize of war. After the war, they were purchased by a Mr. Ryhiner, a merchant of Charleston, who returned them to their home.

In June 1862, the bells were sent for safekeeping to Columbia, South Carolina, where they were destroyed by Sherman's wanton army. Fragments of metal were recovered, however, and sent to Mears & Stainbank of London—the original founders—who, using the original molds, were able to recast the bells. They were installed in St. Michael's in March 1867.

The original chancel window, shattered by shells in 1865, has been replaced by a beautiful Tiffany window, *St. Michael Slaying the Dragon*, from a painting by Raphael.

In the southeast corner of the middle aisle stands the original pulpit, with a sounding board supported by two Corinthian columns. The impressive organ was imported from England in 1768 and is thought to be one of the oldest of its type in this country.

The pew known as the "Governor's Pew" has been occupied by many prominent worshippers, including George Washington and Robert E. Lee.

Visitors to St. Michael's churchyard may be surprised to see the headboard of a bed used as a grave marker. It was placed there in 1770 by William Luyten, who was too poor to buy a stone to mark the grave of his wife, Ann.

Also buried in the churchyard are two of the four South Carolina signers of the Federal Constitution (1787): John Rutledge (1739–1800) and Charles Cotesworth Pinckney (1746–1825).

ST. PHILIP'S CHURCH

142 Church Street. Office open Monday through Thursday, 8:30 a.m. to 4:30 p.m.; Friday, 8:30 a.m. to 1 p.m. Sanctuary hours Monday through Thursday,

10 a.m. to 4 p.m.; Friday, 10 a.m. to 1 p.m. Phone: (843) 722-7734. St. Philip's is the oldest Episcopal congregation in the Carolinas. The first church, a small black cypress structure on a brick foundation, was built in 1681–1682 on the site now occupied by St. Michael's (southeast corner of Meeting and Broad Streets).

The second St. Philip's—built on the present Church Street site in 1723—was a brick building with three porticoes and an octagonal domed tower. It was here, in 1736, that British theologian-evangelist John Wesley preached during his visit to America. George Washington attended Sunday morning

St. Philip's Church, Charleston (LIBRARY OF CONGRESS, PRINTS AND PHOTOGRAPHS DIVISION)

services here on May 8, 1791, and President James Monroe visited on May 2, 1819. The Right Reverend Robert Smith, the first bishop of the Episcopal Diocese of South Carolina, administered policy and officiated at services at the second St. Philip's. The church caught fire in 1796 and was saved from destruction by a Black boatman, who was rewarded with his freedom. But in February 1835 a conflagration raged out of control, razing St. Philip's and nearby structures.

The third and present edifice, which opened for services May 3, 1838, is similar in design to the second church, although a chancel was added and a 200-foot-high steeple replaced the tower. During the War between the States, ten Union shells penetrated St. Philip's, wrecking the chancel and demolishing the organ. The bells were removed to be melted down and recast into cannon.

Among the prominent persons buried in the churchyard are Robert Johnson (the first royal governor of South Carolina), Edward Rutledge (a signer of the Declaration of Independence), Colonel William Rhett (captor of the infamous pirate Stede Bonnet), Christopher Gadsden (a delegate to the Continental Congress and later a lieutenant-governor of South Carolina), and John C. Calhoun (vice president under John Quincy Adams).

UNITARIAN CHURCH

4 Archdale Street. Open Tuesday through Sunday, 9 a.m. to 2 p.m. Phone: (843) 723-4617. This is the home of the oldest Unitarian congregation in the South. The church was under construction at the beginning of the War of Independence. During the occupation of Charleston, British soldiers were quartered here; later, the building was used as a stable. After the war, the church was completed and dedicated in 1787. The entire interior was remodeled during the 1850s under the supervision of architect Francis D. Lee. The interior, with its fan-tracery vaulting, was patterned after that of the Chapel of Henry VII at Westminster Abbey, England.

The stained-glass chancel window, dating from the 1780s, is one of the finest in Charleston. The upper panes depict the four Evangelists— Matthew, Mark, Luke, and John. The lower panel shows Aaron and Moses standing beside the Ark of the Covenant.

WASHINGTON SQUARE

Broad, Meeting, and Chalmers Streets. In this pleasant park, which adjoins City Hall, stand several noteworthy monuments.

The first statue (relocated) installed in this park was to honor the British statesman William Pitt the Elder (1708–1778). It was erected by the grateful citizens of Charleston for his speeches in Parliament against the Stamp Act, speeches that ultimately led to the repeal of that hated legislation. In 1766, the Commons House of Assembly voted a £1,000 commission to sculptor Joseph Wilton to create an appropriate work. Dedicated in 1770, the Pitt statue was first placed at the intersection of Broad and Meeting Streets. After an arm was destroyed during the British bombardment of 1780, the statue was moved to the yard of the old Orphan House on Calhoun Street and was later transplanted to the Charleston County Judicial Center in 2002.

A second statue celebrates native South Carolina poet Henry Timrod (1828–1867); it was designed by E. Valentine and erected in 1901.

A third monument, dedicated to the Washington Light Infantry (a nineteenth-century military unit named for George Washington), was erected in the 1890s.

WHITE POINT GARDENS (THE BATTERY)

2 Murray Boulevard (confluence of the Ashley and Cooper Rivers). A small fortification occupied this site during the War of Independence, when the British fleet and the bombardment of the city forced Charleston's surrender.

In 1838, the area was transformed into a promenade with gardens, which became a popular place for stylishly dressed Charlestonians to spend a Sunday afternoon. During the Civil War, earthworks were built and batteries were erected once again to command the harbor.

Revolutionary War Cannon

Opposite Church Street. This four-pounder is said to have been used in the defense of Charleston in 1780.

Sergeant Jasper Statue

Center walkway. During the Battle of Sullivan's Island on June 28, 1776, Sergeant William Jasper leaped outside the walls to recover the flag from the battered flagstaff and, fastening it to a pole, raised it again above Fort Sullivan (Moultrie).

Pirate Marker

South Battery. In the second decade of the eighteenth century, Charleston shipping was preyed on by marauding buccaneers. It was on this spot that gallows were erected to execute and display captured pirates as a warning to others. The notorious Stede Bonnet, ally of Blackbeard, and his crew met their end here in 1718.

Simms Monument

Center walkway. This monument honors William Gilmore Simms (1806–1870), native poet, novelist, and historian. His romances of

Revolutionary times include *The Partisan* (1835), *The Forayers* (1855), and *Eutaw* (1856). His biographies of Revolutionary War leaders Francis Marion (1844) and Nathanael Greene (1849) remain valuable reference sources.

Brooke Rifle Cannon
Murray Boulevard. This is an example of the powerful artillery pieces developed during the Civil War by John Mercer Brooke, a scientist and naval officer.

Union Cannon
Facing Murray Boulevard. These four cannon were brought from Fort Pitt, Pennsylvania, by Union troops for the bombardment of Fort Sumter, which began in October 1863.

IMPORTANT COLONIAL HOUSES
During March and April, many of these houses may be open to the public through a series of tours. Details can be obtained from the Historic Charleston Foundation, 40 East Bay Street, or call (843) 723-1623. Information is also available at the gift shop at 51 Meeting Street.

BEE HOUSE
94 Church Street. This brick town house was built in the 1730s by Thomas Bee, a delegate to two Continental Congresses and a member from 1776 to 1782 of the South Carolina House of Representatives. He also participated in several military campaigns during the Revolutionary War. In 1790, George Washington appointed him United States District Judge for South Carolina in gratitude for his service to state and nation. The property was later purchased by Governor Joseph Alston, whose wife was Theodosia Burr, celebrated daughter of Aaron Burr, vice president under Thomas Jefferson.

In this house John C. Calhoun, Robert Hayne, and several other political leaders wrote the first draft of the Ordinance of Nullification. This ordinance, passed by the South Carolina legislature in defiance of the federal Tariff Act of 1832, was an affirmation of the principle of states' rights. Its adoption precipitated a constitutional crisis, and President Andrew Jackson responded with a strongly worded proclamation threatening to send troops to the port of Charleston and asserting the power of the federal government over individual states.

BREWTON HOUSE

7 King Street. This magnificent Georgian mansion was built between 1765 and 1769 by Miles Brewton, a prosperous Charleston merchant The design is attributed to architect Ezra Waite. Brewton had been a member of the Commons House of the Colonial legislature for ten years After he and his family were lost at sea on their way to Philadelphia in 1775, the house was inherited by his sisters. One of the sisters, Mrs Rebecca Motte, was residing here at the time of the British occupation.

General Henry Clinton and Lieutenant Colonel Francis Rawdon selected this house for their headquarters. At the insistence of the British, Mrs. Motte reluctantly presided at the table but is said to have kept her three daughters sequestered in the garret. During the Civil War, Union Generals George Meade and Edward Hatch occupied the house (1864–1865).

BRITISH STAFF QUARTERS

15 Legare Street. Built by John Fullerton in the early 1770s, the house was commandeered by the British from 1780 to 1782. Officers on the staffs of Generals Cornwallis and Clinton were quartered here. (The generals lodged at the Brewton House, 27 King Street. At that time, a pathway led from the Brewton House through a postern gate to 15 Legare.)

GIBBES HOUSE

64 South Battery. This handsome Georgian house was built in 1772–1773 by William Gibbes, a wealthy shipowner and merchant who fought in the War of Independence. In 1800, the new owner, Mrs. Sarah Moore Smith, added a marble staircase to the exterior and ornamented the interior in the fashionable Adam style. (Mrs. Washington A. Roebling, widow of the builder of the Brooklyn Bridge, resided here in the 1930s.)

IZARD HOUSE

1 Meeting Street. His Excellency James Glen, governor of the province, occupied this early Georgian house in 1750. Since 1756, it has been occupied by the descendants of the distinguished Izard family. Walter and Ralph Izard were Patriots during the Revolutionary War. (Ralph Izard later served in Congress, 1782–1783.) Their sister Sally was the wife of the royal governor, Lord William Campbell. Another sister, Polly, married Arthur Middleton, a signer of the Declaration of Independence.

THE PINK HOUSE

17 Chalmers Street. This structure (c. 1695–1710), built of West Indian coral stone, served as a pre–Revolutionary War tavern. In the 1750s, Thomas Coker was the proprietor of the tavern, which was a popular haunt of sailors from the nearby harbor. The building faced what was then called Mulatto Alley, a street lined with bordellos. Soon after 1800, when the Charleston City Council launched a campaign to rid the area of undesirable elements, the Pink House was bought for use as a private home.

RAINBOW ROW

3–107 East Bay Street. These brightly colored row houses, built in the mid-eighteenth century, were occupied by merchants during the Revolutionary War. The first floor was used for business and the upper floor for living quarters. Since no interior stairways were constructed, the second floor had to be reached by an outside staircase.

RAMSAY HOUSE

92 Broad Street. In this three-story house lived Dr. David Ramsay (1749–1815), a surgeon who selflessly cared for the wounded during the Revolutionary War. A member of the South Carolina legislature, he was incarcerated when the British captured the city in 1780 and later was sent with other political prisoners to be held at Fort San Marcos in St. Augustine. After his release, he wrote *A History of the Revolution of South Carolina from a British Colony to an Independent State.* Dr. Ramsay served as a member of Congress (1782–1786) and as president of the South Carolina

Senate (1792, 1794, 1796). This distinguished leader, who was assassinated in the spring of 1815, was deeply mourned by the people of his state.

ROYAL GOVERNOR'S RESIDENCE (DANIEL HUGER HOUSE)

34 Meeting Street. This imposing brick house, owned by Daniel Blake, served as the residence of the last royal governor of South Carolina. It is believed that on September 13, 1776, Captain Adam McDonald, a soldier in the Patriot army, disguised himself as a British soldier, deceived Royal Governor William Campbell, and obtained plans concerning the deployment of Loyalist forces.

The next night, Patriot forces assembled at Gadsden's Wharf (at the foot of present-day Calhoun Street) to launch a secret attack on Fort Johnson, the British fortification commanding the southern approach to Charleston Harbor. Campbell, realizing he was in danger and understanding that his authority had been significantly diminished, stealthily slipped out of this house and, escaping to a ship anchored in the harbor, took with him the great seal of the province.

RUTLEDGE HOUSE

116 Broad Street. Currently an inn; call for reservations. Phone: (843) 723-7999. This dwelling was originally owned by John Rutledge, who served as president of South Carolina during the period of the Revolutionary War (1776–1783). He also was a delegate (1765) to the Stamp Act Congress, served as a member of the Continental Congress (1774–1775), and played an important role in drafting the United States Constitution, afterward attending the state ratifying convention (1788). Rutledge was appointed an associate justice of the US Supreme Court (1789–1791).

John Rutledge, artist unknown (LIBRARY OF CONGRESS, PRINTS AND PHOTOGRAPHS DIVISION)

William Washington House, Charleston (LIBRARY OF CONGRESS, PRINTS AND PHOTO-GRAPHS DIVISION)

WILLIAM WASHINGTON HOUSE

8 South Battery. This house was owned by William Washington (1752–1810), a cousin of George Washington. Born in Virginia, William Washington had distinguished himself in battle at Trenton and Princeton before he was sent to South Carolina as a lieutenant colonel. He led his regiments to victory over the British at Cowpens but was captured at Eutaw Springs.

After the war, he and his wife, Jane Elliott, moved into this fine two-story house (built in 1768 by Thomas Savage). According to legend, Jane made the flag that William Washington's cavalry unit carried into battle at Eutaw Springs (September 8, 1781).

NON-REVOLUTIONARY SITES OF INTEREST
CABBAGE ROW
89–91 Church Street. This group of buildings was once populated by poor Black families, who called it "Cabbage Row." Charleston-born DuBose Heyward (1885–1940) used this setting (calling it "Catfish Row") for his novel *Porgy* (1925), which was adapted into a play and then by George Gershwin into an opera, *Porgy and Bess* (1935).

THE CHARLESTON MUSEUM
360 Meeting Street. Open Monday through Saturday, 9 a.m. to 5 p.m.; Sunday, 12 p.m. to 5 p.m. One-site ticket $15, two-site ticket $22, three-site ticket $30; children (under 12) $6, youth (13–17) $12. Phone: (843) 722-2996. Founded in 1773, this is one of the oldest museums in the nation. It displays a fine collection of the early arts and crafts of South Carolina as well as splendid pieces of furniture, unusual examples of textiles, and woodwork paneling salvaged from old houses. Also worth visiting are the exhibits in the Lowcountry History Hall, Historic Silver, and Charleston in the Revolution.

CITY HALL
80 Broad Street. Open Monday through Friday, 8:30 a.m. to 5 p.m. Phone: (843) 577-6970. This is the second-oldest city hall in the United States. It was designed by Charlestonian Gabriel Manigault and was erected in 1801 on the site of the marketplace, a large square where produce from nearby plantations was offered for sale. On December 14, 1782, when the British evacuated Charleston, Patriot troops assembled here as they prepared to once again take control of the city.

Today, visitors to the Council Chamber can see the following paintings: John Trumbull's *George Washington* (1792), Edward Savage's *John Huger* (1787), Rembrandt Peale's *Christopher Gadsden* (c. 1795), Samuel F. B. Morse's *James Monroe* (1819–1820), John Vanderlyn's *Andrew Jackson* (1824), and Charles Fraser's *The Marquis de Lafayette* (1825).

City Hall stands on one of the "Corners of the Four Laws" named by Robert Ripley, author of *Believe It or Not!* On each of the four corners of the intersection of Broad and Meeting Streets is a structure representing an aspect of law: St. Michael's Church (ecclesiastical law); the United States Post Office and the Federal Court (federal law); the courthouse (state law); and the City Hall (city law).

GIBBES MUSEUM OF ART

135 Meeting Street. Open Monday through Tuesday, 10 a.m. to 5 p.m.; Wednesday, 10 a.m. to 8 p.m.; Thursday through Saturday, 10 a.m. to 5 p.m.; Sunday, 1 p.m. to 5 p.m. Adults $12, children (under 3) free, youth (4–17) $6, seniors $10, students $10. Phone: (843) 722-2706. Formerly known as the Gibbes Art Gallery. This imposing structure, built in 1904, houses an excellent collection of American paintings, including works by Benjamin West, Samuel F. B. Morse, Washington Allston, Charles Willson Peale, and Gilbert Stuart. The museum is also noted for its outstanding collection of Japanese prints and Oriental art objects. It is the headquarters of the Carolina Art Association.

HUGUENOT CHURCH

136 Church Street. Open Monday through Thursday, 9 a.m. to 4 p.m. Phone: (843) 722-4385. The present Gothic church, the fourth structure on this site since 1687, was designed by E. B. White. Completed in 1845, it was the place of worship for many persons of French descent who had settled in the surrounding countryside. At one time, church services were scheduled so that parishioners could sail down the Cooper River on the ebb tide and return home on the flood tide. Services were held in French until 1828.

HUNLEY MUSEUM

1250 Supply Street. Open Saturday, 10 a.m. to 5 p.m.; Sunday, 10 a.m. to 3 p.m. Adults $18, children (under 5) free, youth (6–17) $10, seniors $15, students $10, members $12. Phone: (843) 743-4865. The Hunley Museum is supported by the Friends of the Hunley and the South Carolina Hunley Commission. One of the most fascinating exhibits is a replica of the *Hunley,* the first military submarine to sink an enemy ship—the federal sloop-of-war *Housatonic* on February 17, 1864.

KAHAL KADOSH BETH ELOHIM

90 Hasell Street. Open Monday–Friday, 10 a.m.–3 p.m., and Sunday, 12 p.m.–3 p.m. Fee for guided tours: adults $15; youth (5–17) $5; children (under 5), students, and military, free. Phone: (843) 723-1090. This is one of the oldest synagogues in the country. The first synagogue built on this site in 1792 was destroyed by fire in 1838. The present structure, in the Greek Doric style, was finished two years later.

In 1824, the congregation of Beth Elohim became the first Jewish Reform congregation in the United States.

MANIGAULT HOUSE

350 Meeting Street. Open Monday through Saturday, 10 a.m. to 5 p.m.; Sunday, 12 p.m. to 5 p.m. One-site ticket $15, two-site ticket $22, three-site ticket $30; children (3–12) $6, youth (13–17) $12. Phone: (843) 722-2996. An outstanding example of Adam architecture, this mansion was built in 1803 by Joseph Manigault and designed by his brother Gabriel, a planter and amateur architect. The east end of the dining room terminates in a segmental concave, and the curvature is echoed at the west end of the building by a bowed piazza, giving the structure rigid symmetry. The interior is noted for its decorative cornices and ceilings, elaborately carved mantels, and an impressive unsupported circular staircase.

The furnishings include a fine chest-on-chest (in the bedroom) made by Charleston cabinetmaker Thomas Elfe, a twelve-panel coromandel screen (in the entrance hall), a Beauvais tapestry (in the card room), an eighteenth-century boulle clock (in the dining room), two Louis XV commodes with ormolu mounts and marble tops (in the upstairs drawing room), and a portrait (in the drawing room) of Mrs. Peter Manigault, mother of Joseph and Gabriel, painted in 1757 by Jeremiah Theus.

MARKET HALL

188 Meeting Street. Open Thursday through Sunday, 11 a.m. to 4 p.m. Adults $10, children (under 5) free, youth (6–12) $3, military free. Phone: (843) 723-1541. Constructed in 1841 on land originally owned by Charles Cotesworth Pinckney (an important political leader of the Revolutionary period), this building—with its four imposing Doric columns and decorative frieze—is now used by the United Daughters of the Confederacy as a chapter hall. It also houses a museum exhibiting memorabilia of the Confederacy.

OLD SLAVE MART MUSEUM

6 Chalmers Street. Open Monday through Saturday, 9 a.m. to 5 p.m. General admission $8, children (under 6) free, youth (7–12) $7, seniors $7, students $7, military $7. Phone: (843) 724-3732. In 1856, Thomas Ryan and Son, brokers, purchased this building for an auction mart. About thirty brokers sold slaves, livestock, and furniture here. Slaves were housed in nearby buildings before the sale. Some historians estimate that as many as 80,000 Africans had been imported into the colonies by the time of the Revolution. When the British evacuated Charleston, they confiscated 5,000 slaves to be sold in Florida and Jamaica.

Since 1938, the Old Slave Market has been a museum dedicated to these events.

RUSSELL HOUSE

51 Meeting Street. Open Monday, 1 p.m. to 4 p.m.; Tuesday through Sunday, 10 a.m. to 4 p.m. Adults $16, children (under 5) free, youth (6–16) $7. Phone: (843) 724-8481. Nathaniel Russell, a native of Rhode Island who settled in Charleston in the late 1760s and became a prosperous merchant, built this luxurious house (designed by architect Russell Warren) in 1809 at a cost of $80,000.

This magnificent mansion is distinguished by the two unusual elliptical rooms, the spiral free-flying staircase, the beautifully carved woodwork, and the exquisite furniture. Among the important furnishings are an Aubusson rug (c. 1800), an early nineteenth-century Italian table with a scagliola top, a harp made by Sébastien Érard in 1803, a pair of lyreback chairs made in Baltimore, a Chamberlain Worcester tea service (c. 1800), and a Regency bronze-and-ormolu clock.

The Russell family resided here until 1857, when the house was sold to the governor of South Carolina, Robert F. W. Allston.

JOINT BASE CHARLESTON

Travel north along East Bay Street. Formerly known as the United States Naval Base, it provides support to various military and related federal agencies. It is home to thousands of active-duty and reserve units.

Tours are available April 1 to November 1, Tuesday through Thursday, 9 a.m. to 2:30 p.m. Hours may vary. Tours must be reserved in advance. Phone: (843) 963-5608.

RECOMMENDED SIDE TRIPS

BOONE HALL PLANTATION

1235 Long Point Road. Open Monday through Saturday, 9 a.m. to 5 p.m.; Sunday, 12 p.m. to 5 p.m. General admission $30, children (under 5) free, youth (6–12) $12, seniors $27, military $27, AAA $27. Phone: (843) 884-4371.

Boone Hall Plantation was the property of John Boone, one of the earliest settlers in South Carolina, who received this land as a grant in 1681 from the Lords Proprietors. It became a thriving cotton plantation of 17,000 acres.

A magnificent three-quarter-mile avenue of huge moss-draped oaks leads to the main house, which was renovated in 1935. Visitors can also see nine small structures that were used as slave quarters. The formal gardens and pecan groves add to the beauty of this estate, which was used in the filming of *Gone with the Wind*.

CHARLES TOWNE LANDING PARK

1500 Old Town Road. Open daily, 9 a.m. to 5 p.m. Hours may vary. A visitor center offers information and contains a museum. Admission fees to the park are adults $12, youth (6–15) $7, seniors $7. Phone: (843) 852-4200. Hiking and biking trails are available. Check hours and safety regulations.

In this park is the site of the first settlement of Charleston. In 1670, three small ships with 140 English men and women landed here—on the western bank of the Ashley River—and built a settlement they named Albemarle Point (for Lord Proprietor George Monk, the first Duke of Albemarle). Soon afterward, the settlement was renamed Charles Towne in honor of the king.

During the spring of 1680, the government and many colonists moved across the river to a new site, on which the present-day city of Charleston grew.

Charles Towne Landing is part of a 184-acre park administered by the state of South Carolina.

CHARLES TOWNE LANDING

Major points of interest:

Reconstructed palisade walls marking the approximate location of the early settlement.

Full-scale replica of the *Adventure*, a seventeenth-century trading vessel used by the colonists. Visitors may board the ketch, now moored in the lagoon.

Crop garden with the same variety of plants that settlers grew.

Pavilion with exhibitions describing the development of Colonial South Carolina. Artifacts discovered here are on display.

Wildlife sanctuary with various types of animals indigenous to this region in the seventeenth and eighteenth centuries. Some species are now almost extinct.

SULLIVAN'S ISLAND

2056 Middle Street, Town of Sullivan's Island. Phone: (843) 883-3198.

The original fort on this island, Fort Sullivan, was constricted in the shape of a square with a bastion at each corner. Built of palmetto logs placed in two parallel rows sixteen feet apart—the space between filled with sand—the fort was armed with thirty-one guns (ranging from nine-pounders to twenty-six-pounders).

FORT MOULTRIE / FORT SULLIVAN

1214 Middle Street. Open daily, 9 a.m. to 4:30 p.m. General admission $10.

On June 28, 1776, the British fleet under Admiral Peter Parker attacked the Patriot-held fort, commanded by Colonel William Moultrie. Instead of shattering the fort's walls, the shells from the British ships buried themselves in the fibrous palmetto logs. Moultrie's cannon damaged several ships and forced one man-of-war to run aground.

Under the cover of night, the British withdrew; five weeks later, the entire fleet sailed north. A grateful South Carolina Assembly passed a resolution giving old Fort Sullivan a new name—Fort Moultrie.

But early in 1780 the enemy fleet, commanded by Admiral Mariot Arbuthnot, reappeared off Charleston. At daybreak on May 3, 200 men, led by Captain Charles Hudson of His Majesty's frigate *Richmond*, made an unopposed landing on Sullivan's Island, and the besieged fort was forced to surrender. This was a major defeat, leading to the British occupation of Charleston.

Fort Moultrie was reoccupied by the Americans on December 14, 1782. When President George Washington visited Charleston in 1791, he toured Sullivan's Island accompanied by General Moultrie and other distinguished citizens. By that time, Fort Moultrie had been abandoned and had fallen into disrepair.

The present brick fort was built between 1807 and 1811. The original walls and the magazines are still intact, although the barracks were destroyed during the Civil War. On December 26, 1860, Major Robert

Exterior walls of Fort Moultrie, Sullivan's Island (ALPER)

Anderson—fearing attack from the Confederate forces who lay claim to federal property in the area—moved the small garrison he commanded at Fort Moultrie to Fort Sumter out in the harbor. Fort Moultrie had served as an army post until 1947, when it was deactivated.

Main points of interest:

Outside the **Entrance Gate** visitors may see the grave of Seminole leader Osceola (c. 1800–1838), who was confined here in 1838 because he had opposed the US government's plans to relocate the Indians. He died several months after his imprisonment.

The **Guardrooms** flanking the main entrance.

The **Munitions Magazine** and **Battery Bingham** (a two-gun battery built in 1899), **Battery McCorkie** (a 1901 battery with three guns), and **Battery Lord** (with several rapid-fire guns mounted in 1903 to protect the harbor).

The **Main Storage Magazine** of two rooms, built in 1837.

The **1809 Powder Magazine**, the oldest structure in the fort.

The **Twelve-Pounder Field Cannon** used during the Civil War.

FORT SUMTER NATIONAL MONUMENT

Fort Sumter is on an island in Charleston Harbor and can be reached only by boat. Tours tickets are available through Fort Sumter Tours and depart from Liberty Square and Patriot's Point. Adults $43, children $26. Phone: (843) 722-2628.

This five-sided brick-and-stone fortification was constructed between 1829 and 1860. Named for South Carolina's Revolutionary War hero Thomas Sumter (1734–1832), it was armed with 135 guns and garrisoned 650 men.

After the Ordinance of Secession was passed (December 20, 1860), South Carolina demanded all federal property within its borders, particularly the forts in Charleston Harbor. On December 26, Major Robert Anderson removed his US Army command from Fort Moultrie to the stronger defensive site of Fort Sumter. When President James Buchanan refused to order Anderson's evacuation, the governor of South Carolina, F. W. Pickens, ordered guns from nearby forts aimed directly at Fort Sumter.

On January 9, 1861, an unarmed merchant vessel, *Star of the West,* which was sent to reinforce the Fort Sumter garrison, was driven back by the fire of South Carolina guns. Three months later, while newly inaugurated President Abraham Lincoln was considering action to provision the beleaguered fort, it was fired on by Confederate guns (April 12). After a thirty-four-hour bombardment, Anderson and his men agreed to withdraw. The next day, President Lincoln called for 75,000 men, and the Civil War had begun.

In 1863, Union naval attacks on the fort were repulsed. Not until 1865, when General Sherman forced the evacuation of Charleston, was the United States flag once again raised above the fort.

Main points of interest:

Left Flank Gun Rooms. In the gun rooms of the lower tier are mounted two guns on casemate carriages: One is a rifled and banded forty-two-pounder; the other is a forty-two-pound smooth bore.

Enlisted Men's Barracks. This three-story building had a kitchen and mess facilities on the ground floor and sleeping quarters on the upper stories.

Officers' Quarters. Besides serving as a lodging for officers, this structure contained storerooms, administrative offices, powder magazines, and a guardhouse.

Left Face. Only the ruins remain of the left-face brick casemates that were destroyed by Union guns during the Civil War.

Right Face. Guns mounted on the lower tier were involved in the initial exchange of fire with Fort Moultrie on April 12–14, 1861.

Right Gorge Angle. On April 12, 1861, Captain Abner Doubleday, using a gun mounted on the first tier, was the first from Fort Sumter to return fire.

Union Garrison Monument. The US government erected this monument in 1932 in memory of the garrison defending Fort Sumter. The names of the soldiers manning the fort are listed on a tablet.

Museum. Exhibits dramatically re-create the historical events associated with Fort Sumter.

MAGNOLIA GARDENS

3550 Ashley River Road, on Route 61. Open daily, 9 a.m. to 5 p.m. Closed Thanksgiving, December 25, and January 1. Adults $32, children (under 4) free, youth (5–13) $16, seniors $29, military $29. Phone: (843) 571-1266.

This estate, formerly called "Magnolia-on-the-Ashley," has been the residence of the celebrated Drayton family since 1671.

The Draytons have been active in South Carolina public affairs since Revolutionary times. William Henry Drayton (1742–1779), a brilliant orator, served as president of the Provincial Congress and a member of the Continental Congress. His son John (1767–1822) was a governor of the state (1800–1802, 1808–1810). During the War of 1812, Colonel William Drayton (1776–1846) commanded Fort Moultrie.

When, in the second decade of the nineteenth century, there was no direct male heir, the property passed to the son of the Draytons' oldest daughter, John Grimké Drayton. He was an ordained minister, but, because of ill health, he retired to this estate, where he devoted his time to cultivating these beautiful gardens.

In 1843, Grimké Drayton began importing *Camellia japonica*; later he planted the first *Azalea indica* in the United States. This magnificent twenty-five-acre garden now has almost 700 varieties of camellias and many types of azaleas, as well as examples of *Magnolia grandiflora*, Chinese yew, and French cypress.

DRAYTON HALL

The Colonial brick mansion that once stood on these grounds was used by Lord Cornwallis as temporary headquarters. Soon after the Revolutionary War, Drayton Hall was accidentally destroyed by fire. A second structure, built of cypress, was razed by Union troops during the Civil War. The present house was completed in the late 1860s.

MIDDLETON PLACE GARDENS

4300 Ashley River Road. Open daily, 9 a.m. to 5 p.m.; December 24, 9 a.m. to 1 p.m. Closed December 25. Adults $29, children (under 5) free, youth (6–13) $10, students $15. Phone: (843) 556-6020. Secondary phone: (800) 782-3608.

These gardens were the property of the Middleton family, renowned for their service to the state and nation. Henry Middleton (1717–1784) served as one of the presidents of the Continental Congress, and his son Arthur (1742–1787) was a signer of the Declaration of Independence. Arthur's son Henry (1770–1846) became a governor of South Carolina (1810–1812) and a US congressman (1815–1819).

In 1740, Henry Middleton sent to England for a landscape gardener to design the formal gardens and ornamental lakes for his estate. It took almost ten years to complete the project. The forty acres—a series of terraces that descend from the bluff of the Ashley River—are noted for their stately oak trees and magnificent azaleas and camellias. The first camellias brought to America were planted here in 1787.

MIDDLETON MANSION

The original brick mansion, built in 1741, was looted and burned by Sherman's army as it marched from Savannah to Columbia. Only one wing remains, and it has been restored. Visitors can view a fine collection of family portraits and furniture. The plantation stable yards have been renovated and are now used as workshops to display Colonial crafts such as candle making and weaving.

Georgetown

REVOLUTIONARY WAR HISTORY

The third-oldest town in South Carolina, Georgetown was settled in 1734–1735. Surrounded by prosperous indigo and rice plantations, the town had become a thriving port by the middle of the eighteenth century.

When the nineteen-year-old Lafayette arrived from France on June 13, 1777, to join the Patriot cause, he and his companions disembarked from their ship *Victoire* at North Island across the bay from Georgetown.

VISITOR INFORMATION

Tourist information is available from the **Georgetown Chamber of Commerce**, 531 Front Street; (843) 546-8436.

GUIDED TOURS

Cap'n Rod's Lowcountry Tours, (843) 477-0287
Swamp Fox Tours, (843) 527-1112
Georgetown Fishing Charters, (843) 477-0287
PUBLIC TRANSPORTATION Regional bus transportation is provided by Coast RTA. For information and schedules, call (843) 488-0865 or visit www.CoastRTA.com.

Soon after the British occupied Charleston in 1780, they established a small garrison at Georgetown. An attempt by the Patriots to regain control of the town in November 1780 ended in failure. In January 1781, forces under the command of Francis Marion and Henry ("Light-Horse Harry") Lee attacked the post, but, because of a shortage of ammunition, they were forced to abandon the attempt. Four months later,

Marion, learning that the garrison had been reduced to roughly eighty soldiers, gathered a large corps of militiamen and marched to Georgetown. On their arrival, they were overjoyed to discover that during the night the British had fled to Charleston by ship. With the garrison under Marion's control, Georgetown and the countryside were free of British domination.

COLONIAL AND REVOLUTIONARY WAR SITES
BOLEN-BELLUME HOUSE
222 Broad Street. Not open to the public. During the British occupation of Georgetown, this two-story frame house served as the headquarters for senior staff officers.

HOPSEWEE PLANTATION
494 Hopsewee Road. Open Tuesday through Saturday, 10 a.m. to 3 p.m. Historic Landmark House Tour tickets for adults $24, children (6–11) $10, youth (12–17) $15, seniors $22. Hopsewee Historic Museum tickets for adults $15, children (6–11) $5, youth (12–17) $8, seniors $13. Phone: (843) 546-7891. A typical Lowcountry plantation house of the mid-eighteenth century, Hopsewee has on each floor four rooms opening onto a central hallway. The house is noted for its elaborate hand-carved molding and fine period furniture. This was the home of Thomas Lynch (1727–1776) and Thomas Lynch Jr. (1749–1779), both delegates to the Continental Congress. The son's presence at the Congress has been recorded for all ages through his signature on the Declaration of Independence. Thomas Sr. died before the document was signed.

KAMINSKI HOUSE
1003 Front Street. Open Monday through Saturday, 11 a.m. to 5 p.m., with tours at 11 a.m., 1 p.m., and 3 p.m. Adults $12, children (under 5) free, youth (6–17) $6, seniors $10, members free. Phone: (843) 546-7706. This outstanding mansion was built in 1760 by Benjamin Allston, a rector of Prince George Winyah Church. It was willed to the city of Georgetown by his great-great-granddaughter, Mrs. Harold Kaminski, and opened to the public. The house is furnished with fine antiques, including a

pair of acajou French Empire side chairs, a rare Baluchistan rug, sixteen matched Duncan Phyfe chairs, a silver coffeepot (c. 1790) made by Garrett Schanck, and an unusual Hepplewhite letter cabinet.

PAWLEY-PARKER HOUSE

1019 Front Street. Not open to the public. Local historians believe that Washington stayed overnight in this house on his way to Charleston in 1791. Arriving on Saturday, April 30, he was greeted by a cannon salute, a company of infantry, and cheering crowds. In the late afternoon, he attended a banquet given in his honor. The house (with the front originally facing toward the Sampit River) was built about 1760; the two bay windows facing Front Street are later additions.

PRINCE GEORGE WINYAH CHURCH

300 Broad Street. Sunday service 7:45 a.m., 9 a.m., and 11:15 a.m. Service times subject to change. Phone: (843) 546-4358. Founded in 1721, this parish was named for the son of King George II. The brick church was constructed between 1737 and 1750; the belfry was added in 1824. The English stained-glass window behind the altar was originally part of St. Mary's Church for African Americans at Hagley Plantation in Waccamaw. It is believed that the British used this church as a stable during the occupation of Georgetown. In the nearby cemetery are graves of Revolutionary and Confederate soldiers.

RICE MUSEUM

633 Front Street. Open Tuesday through Saturday, 11 a.m. to 4 p.m. Adults $9, children (under 5) free, youth (6–21) $5, seniors $7. Phone: (843) 546-7423. Located in the Old Market Building (erected about 1835), the Rice Museum is devoted to the history of the rice-growing industry in South Carolina. Dioramas, maps, photographs, and exhibits show the importance of the crop to the economic development of the region.

WINYAH INDIGO SOCIETY

509 Prince Street. Open for tours by appointment Monday through Friday 9 a.m. to 5:30 p.m.; Saturday tours available by appointment. Can be booked for special events through www.winyahindigohall.com. Organized in 1740, the Indigo Society was chartered by King George II as a "Convivial Club to meet to talk over the latest news from London."

The first president of the group was Thomas Lynch Sr. Dues were paid in indigo. (Used in the manufacturing of blue dye, the indigo plant was one of South Carolina's main crops, playing an important role in the colony's economic growth.) In 1753, the society established one of the first free schools in America.

The present meeting hall dates from 1857.

IMPORTANT COLONIAL HOUSES

Other fine Colonial houses may still be seen in Georgetown. Although they are not open to the public, tourists to the city who are visiting the neighborhoods in which they are located may take the opportunity to view these dwellings.

Craft-Rodwell House (1749)	*212 Orange Street*
Ford House (1739)	*914 Highmarket Street*
Forster-Schneider House (1760)	*909 Prince Street*
Fraser House (1770)	*1028 Front Street*
Man-Doyle House (1775)	*528 Front Street*
McGrath House (1770)	*220 Queen Street*
Pacey House (1760)	*601 Highmarket Street*
Rumley-Miller House (1760)	*331 Screven Street*
Stewart-Congdon House (1750)	*513 Prince Street*
Tucker-Smith House (1760)	*15 Cannon Street*
Ward-Bull House (1750)	*614 Prince Street*
Withers-Porter House (1740)	*316 Screven Street*

Santee

REVOLUTIONARY WAR HISTORY

An air of complacency hung over the British camp at Eutaw Springs (near Santee) on the morning of September 8, 1781. So certain was Colonel Alexander Stewart of the security of his encampment that he sent a foraging party of 100 unarmed men to bring back fresh food. Little did he suspect that General Nathanael Greene was approaching with a Patriot force of 2,200 soldiers.

Stewart was soon alerted, however, by informers. Fearing an attack, he hurriedly dispatched a reconnoitering patrol under Major John Coffin. They ran directly into the vanguard of Greene's soldiers and suffered heavy losses in the ensuing skirmish. When the retreating Redcoats returned to camp and sounded an alarm, Stewart commanded his men to prepare for battle. A single line of troops was positioned so that the right flank was protected by Eutaw Creek and the left by a dense thicket.

Near the steep bank of Eutaw Creek, nearly 300 men—six companies of grenadiers and light infantry under the command of Major John Marjoribanks—were deployed at an angle to the main line.

The American forces now marshaled for the attack. General Greene ordered the North Carolina militia to the front, Andrew Pickens's South Carolina militia to the left flank, and Francis Marion's South Carolina militia to the right. "Light-Horse Harry" Lee's cavalry stood in readiness at the outer right flank, and Colonel William Washington's cavalry was held in reserve at the rear of the formation. With this military configuration, the Patriots advanced on the enemy.

Fighting raged for nearly three hours. The steady thrust of the first line of militiamen sent the British scurrying in retreat. Only Marjoribanks's detachment remained in position. Colonel Washington and his men then charged into the murderous fire of Marjoribanks's troops. Almost half of Washington's men were killed or wounded, and he was captured.

The remaining Colonial forces pursued the British through the camp. Suddenly the action reversed itself. The hungry, exhausted Patriots fell on the spoils of a still-unachieved victory and began to loot the stores, eating the abandoned provisions and guzzling the liquor. Major Marjoribanks took advantage of this unexpected turn of events and swept down on the plunderers, driving them from the field. Although the assault was successful, he sustained a mortal wound.

When the smoke had cleared over the battleground, the grim tally of casualties was taken: 522 Americans, 866 British (two-fifths of the force). Historians state that this encounter was the last major Revolutionary War battle in the Carolinas, although skirmishes continued.

COLONIAL AND REVOLUTIONARY WAR SITES
EUTAW SPRINGS BATTLEFIELD SITE

1030 15th Street Northwest. Near Eutawville, South Carolina, and accessible from Route 6/45. Phone: (202) 367-1861. Visitors to the battlefield

may retrace the events of September 8, 1781, through several markers and monuments. The most noteworthy are the following:

The Battle Monument

This granite shaft, dedicated to those who fought here, was erected in 1912 by the Eutaw Chapter of the Daughters of the American Revolution.

Grave of Major Marjoribanks and Marker

After British officer John Marjoribanks was wounded, he was carried to Wantoot Plantation (now under nearby Lake

The Battle Monument, Eutaw Springs Battlefield Site, Santee (ALPER)

Moultrie), where he died and was buried on October 22, 1781. His grave and marker were moved here in 1941 by the South Carolina Public Service Authority.

Northampton Marker
This marker calls attention to the residence of General William Moultrie, Northampton Plantation, which was once located near here.

FORT WATSON SITE
Fort Watson is located on the north shore of Lake Marion and is part of the Santee National Wildfire Refuge. From April 15 to April 23, 1781, British and Patriot troops fought here for possession of this garrison. The conflict was stalemated because the Colonials lacked a cannon with which to batter down the walls of the fort. Colonel Hezekiah Maham offered an imaginative suggestion building a tower so that the Patriot soldiers could fire down on their enemy. During the night of April 22, a crude rectangular structure of rough logs was erected.

At dawn, the surprised British discovered a fifty-foot tower looming above the fort manned by American riflemen. As they opened fire, other Patriots, under the commands of Francis Marion and Henry ("Light-Horse Harry") Lee, charged the fort. Unable to repel their adversaries, the British surrendered.

Camden

REVOLUTIONARY WAR HISTORY

After the fall of Charleston in May 1780, the British established a series of posts across the northern section of the colony, with Camden as the principal garrison. To counter the growing British dominance in the Carolinas, Congress selected General Horatio Gates (1728–1806), the hero of Saratoga, to assume command of the Continental troops in the South. His appointment was a serious miscalculation.

Gates reached the camp of Baron de Kalb (Prussian officer who had come to America to fight for the Patriot cause) at Cox's Mill, North Carolina, on July 25, 1780, and immediately issued orders for a march to Camden. De Kalb proposed that they march southwest by way of Salisbury and Charlotte and then to Camden—a circuitous route, but one that would take them through fertile farmland cultivated by people sympathetic to the Revolution. Gates rejected this route in favor of one that was fifty miles shorter, even though it ran through a region that was, for the most part, wilderness and transversed Cross Creek County, an area hostile to the Patriot cause. Little food was available except peaches and green corn; soon intestinal disorders and dysentery were rampant. The march turned into a two-week nightmare as the exhausted, debilitated men trudged toward Camden. On August 13, they arrived at Clermont, South Carolina, several miles north of their objective.

On the night of August 15, Gates prepared to launch a surprise attack against the British. Before the march commenced, he ordered molasses added to the troops' rations to bolster their energy, but this only added to their gastric distress.

That same evening, General Charles Cornwallis, unaware of Gates's plans, ordered a night march to surprise the Continentals. The two armies started moving along the same road toward each other. When the astonished forces encountered each other, they simultaneously opened fire. After the first burst of gunfire, both sides withdrew to await the morning light.

Dawn revealed a thinly studded forest of pines flanked on both sides by swamps. The American line was formed for battle. To the right were stationed Delaware and Maryland Continentals, commanded by Baron de Kalb and General Mordecai Gist, but the center and left were manned by inexperienced militia.

They were no match for the overpowering army of scarlet and steel commanded by Cornwallis, Rawdon, and Tarleton. As the British phalanx advanced on them, the terrified front and left lines threw up their muskets and ran frantically in retreat. Only the Maryland and Delaware veterans remained, locked in conflict with Rawdon's forces. While de Kalb rallied his men, he was seriously wounded and taken prisoner. A final charge by Tarleton's cavalry broke all American resistance. After the battle, Tarleton led a relentless pursuit of the Patriots, surprising them at Fishing Creek and capturing prisoners and supplies.

The craven Gates ignominiously fled the battlefield and did not interrupt his retreat until he reached Charlotte and later rode to Hillsborough, North Carolina—traveling approximately 180 miles from Camden! Baron de Kalb was carried back to Camden, where he died three days later.

The Battle of Camden was one of the worst defeats inflicted on the American army. While the British casualties numbered 324, almost 1,000 Patriot soldiers were killed or wounded.

VISITOR INFORMATION

Revolutionary War Visitor Center, 212 Broad Street. Open Monday–Saturday, 8:30 a.m. to 5 p.m.; Sunday, 1 p.m. to 4:40 p.m. Closed major holidays. Phone: (803) 272-0076.

Camden Chamber of Commerce, 80 Campus Drive; (803) 432-2525

PUBLIC TRANSPORTATION Since Camden does not have an elaborate public transportation system, visitors to the city who do not wish to walk should use automobiles or taxis.

Convenient local bus service is provided by the King Haigler Express, a free limited bus loop that operates 10 a.m. to 4 p.m. on weekdays. Contact @camdensc.org. For regional transportation to nearby towns, call Pee Dee Regional Transport Authority at (843) 665-2227.

TAXI SERVICE Sunshine Taxi LLC, (803) 572-3266; Ride Me Taxi Services, (803) 334-1312

COLONIAL AND REVOLUTIONARY WAR SITES
BETHESDA PRESBYTERIAN CHURCH AND
DE KALB MONUMENT

502 East De Kalb Street. Open Monday through Thursday, 9 a.m. to 4 p.m.; Sunday, 9 a.m. to 5:30 p.m. Phone: (803) 432-4593.

Camden's first Presbyterian meeting hall was destroyed by the British during the Revolutionary War. This structure (the fourth Presbyterian church in the town) was built in 1820 by architect Robert Mills, who designed the Washington Monument.

In front of this graceful Doric-columned church is a monument honoring Baron Johann de Kalb,

Bethesda Presbyterian Church and De Kalb Monument, Camden (LIBRARY OF CONGRESS, PRINTS AND PHOTOGRAPHS DIVISION)

the Prussian general who was mortally wounded (August 1780) while leading Patriot troops in the Battle of Camden. In the midst of the rout of the Patriot troops, the heroic de Kalb, unhorsed and continuing to fight on foot, directed the movements of the Maryland and Delaware troops. According to legend, he fell to the ground only after three musket balls and eight bayonet points had penetrated his body. British officers buried him in an obscure grave, but in 1825 his remains were reinterred in the Bethesda churchyard.

De Kalb's friend and comrade in arms, Lafayette, who was touring the United States in 1824–1825, laid the cornerstone of this monument on March 9, 1825. The monument is composed of twenty-four granite blocks, each representing a state of the Union at that time. The inscription reads, "Here lies the remains of Baron de Kalb—a German by birth, but in principle, a citizen of the world."

CAMDEN BATTLEFIELD SITE AND HISTORIC CAMDEN

Historic Camden administers both the battlefield site and the downtown historic district.

Camden Battlefield Site

1698 Flat Rock Road. Open daylight hours. Free. Can be reached by walking trails or automobile. The site of the Battle of Camden (August 16, 1780) is marked by a monument honoring Prussian-born Baron Johann de Kalb (1721–1780), who sailed to America in 1777 to join the Patriot cause. De Kalb was wounded and captured here and died in Camden three days later. A stone memorial marker was placed here by the Daughters of the American Revolution (DAR) in 1907. A newer tribute to the soldiers who fought at Camden—the America 250 Patriots Marker—was dedicated on March 22, 2023.

Historic Camden Living History Park

Start your visit at the visitor center at 222 Broad Street. Open Tuesday through Saturday, 10 a.m. to 4:30 p.m.; Sunday, 1 p.m. to 4:30 p.m. Guided tours available 11:30 a.m. to 2:30 p.m. Self-guided tour tickets for adults $10; 20 percent discount for youth, seniors, and military. Guided tour tickets

Battle of Camden—Death cf De Kalb (detail), engraving after A. Chappel (THE NATIONAL ARCHIVES, WASHINGTON, �)

for adults $20; 20 percent discount for youth, seniors, military. Phone: (803) 432-9841.

This 107-acre living history park and museum complex offers visitors the opportunity to explore the region's history and culture during the eighteenth century. Military defenses and historic houses can be viewed. Demonstrations and reenactments are scheduled throughout the year.

The oldest existing inland town in South Carolina, Camden was settled during the 1730s when several English families built crude log cabins along the Wateree River. The village was first known as Pine Tree Hill but changed its name to Camden in 1768 in honor of Charles Pratt, Earl of Camden, a member of the British Parliament who championed the rights of the colonies.

Main points of interest:

The Northeast Redoubt. The British erected this redoubt to block the intersection of Lyttleton and Bull Streets. A six-foot-deep ditch surrounded an earthen wall six feet high.

The Southeast Redoubt. This small, isolated earthwork flanked the "Cornwallis House" (Kershaw Mansion) and protected the southeast approach of the town.

Magazine Site. A powder magazine was constructed on this site by the town's residents in 1777. It was a rectangular brick building supported by four buttresses. It was demolished in 1794, but the foundations may still be seen.

Kershaw-Cornwallis Mansion. The Kershaw Mansion was built in 1777 by Camden's leading citizen, Joseph Kershaw, wealthy proprietor of indigo works, a gristmill, tobacco warehouses, and a distillery. During the British occupation of Camden, this house was commandeered and used as headquarters first by Cornwallis and later by Lord Rawdon. In 1865, the residence was destroyed by fire, although it has since been reconstructed.

The Drakeford House. This log cabin was originally located twelve miles north of Camden near Granny's Quarter Creek. Its first owner, Richard Drakeford, was a Virginian who settled in North Carolina around 1754. Both he and his brother fought in the Revolution. When the house was removed to a site in Historic Camden, a mantel, some doors, and floorboards were replaced. Today, the Drakeford House is a small museum displaying Revolutionary War relics, pottery, armaments, and a model of the Kershaw Mansion.

The Craven House. This one-room house was built at 816 Mill Street shortly after the Revolutionary War. All that is known about its owner, John Craven, is that he was an accountant, unmarried, and, according to one legal document, "a lunatic." In 1806, a wealthy merchant and landowner named Zachariah Cantey purchased the property, and his family used the house as a recreation center for card playing and other forms of entertainment.

Moved to the present site in 1970, the structure was restored and furnished with representative period pieces.

HOBKIRK'S HILL BATTLE SITE

The battlefield site is now a residential neighborhood of Camden, but several markers are located throughout the area.

In the spring of 1781, Camden was still occupied by British forces. In late April, General Nathanael Greene arrived in the vicinity with a force of nearly 1,400 Patriot soldiers and encamped along Hobkirk's Hill, a sandy ridge roughly one mile north of Camden. Alerted to Greene's presence, Lord Francis Rawdon marched his troops out and took the Americans by surprise. Disorder reigned in the camp, but lines of battle were quickly formed, and at first the Patriots appeared to be winning. Suddenly the Maryland regiment was thrown into confusion when they mistook an order to regroup for a command to withdraw. Taking advantage of this opportunity, Rawdon's soldiers pressed forward, routing the Americans.

Although Greene was forced to call a retreat, giving the day's victory to Rawdon, the presence of his and other Patriot forces in the area cut off Rawdon's supply lines. On May 9, after unsuccessfully trying to ferret out the ensconced adversary, the British evacuated Camden. As they withdrew, the town was set on fire.

According to local legend, the body of a soldier whose head had been shot off by a cannonball during the battle was carried off by his horse into the nearby swamps. Tradition has it that on certain nights when the fog is dense, the headless ghost, mounted on a skeleton steed, comes out of the swamp and rides around Hobkirk's Hill in a vain search for his head.

Markers

The Hobkirk's Hill Battle Marker, General Greene Marker, American Army Marker, and British Army Marker are all placed along Kirkwood Lane. The Struggle for the Hill Marker and the Counterblow Marker are located near the intersection of Greene and Lyttleton Streets.

QUAKER CEMETERY

713 Meeting Street. Phone: (803) 432-4356. In the mid-eighteenth century, a small Quaker community that had settled here built a meetinghouse and established a cemetery. The Quakers have long since vanished from this area, and their cemetery, much enlarged, now holds the graves of people of other faiths. Dates on the tombstones span a period from pre-Revolutionary times to the present century. Buried here are the following:

> Agnes of Glasgow, who, according to her tombstone, "departed this life February 12, 1780, age 20." Although nothing factual is known of Agnes's life, she is the subject of a romantic legend. The story relates that she was engaged to a lieutenant who was ordered to the colonies during the Revolutionary War. Finding the separation unbearable, she set out to be reunited with him. After a rough sea passage, she arrived in South Carolina, and Loyalists directed the determined young lady to a hospital unit near Camden. She rushed to her stricken lover's side, arriving only to watch him die in her arms. With an agonized shriek, she threw herself across his body and died of a broken heart. (Sticklers for historical detail point out that the British did not arrive in Camden until several months after her death.)

> Dr. Isaac Alexander, who attended the wounded Baron de Kalb.

> Dr. James Martin, a surgeon who fought in the Revolutionary War.

> Richard Kirkland, a young Confederate soldier who gained fame by risking his life to take water to dying Union troops.

> Generals J. B. Kershaw and John D. Kennedy, both heroes of the War between the States.

> Dr. George Todd, brother-in-law of Abraham Lincoln, who was in charge of a hospital here during the Civil War.

> Richard Hobson Hilton and John Cantey Villepigue, both recipients of the Congressional Medal of Honor during World War I.

OTHER REVOLUTIONARY WAR SITES AND IMPORTANT COLONIAL HOUSES

BLUE HOUSE SITE

Northwestern corner of Meeting and Broad Streets. The Blue House was the residence of Dr. Isaac Alexander, who attended the wounded Baron de Kalb here. After his death, de Kalb was buried behind this house. In 1825, his body was reinterred in the Bethesda Presbyterian churchyard.

CARTER-LAFAYETTE HOUSE SITE

1121 Broad Street, Lafayette Hall. The mansion that once stood on this site was in 1825 the home of John Carter, who placed it at the disposal of the visiting Marquis de Lafayette.

CENTRAL SQUARE

Intersection of Bull and Broad Streets. This area was the center of eighteenth-century Camden. George Washington addressed the local citizens here on May 26, 1791, during his tour of the South.

REVOLUTIONARY WAR JAIL SITE

Across Broad Street from the Robert Mills Courthouse. During the Revolutionary War, the small "gaol" here held many political and military prisoners. Among them was the young Andrew Jackson, who was captured by the British during a skirmish near Camden. A local legend relates his defiant refusal to clean the boots of a British officer who, in a vengeful mood, angrily struck Jackson with a saber.

WASHINGTON HOUSE

1413 Mill Street. Not open to the public. This handsome house (originally located at the corner of King and Fair Streets) was the scene of a gala reception held in honor of President Washington during his brief visit to Camden in 1791.

NON-REVOLUTIONARY SITES OF INTEREST
CONFEDERATE GENERALS' MEMORIAL
(THE PANTHEON)

Rectory Square, Chestnut and Lyttleton Streets. This monument of six columns serves as a memorial honoring six Confederate generals from the Camden area:

> James Chestnut, a US senator from South Carolina who resigned to become a delegate to the Secession Convention and later served on the staff of Jefferson Davis.

> Joseph Brevard Kershaw, a prominent lawyer, saw action at Bull Run, Harpers Ferry, Fredericksburg, and Gettysburg.

> John B. Villepigue, a graduate of West Point, died of malaria after only one year of service in the Confederate army.

> James Cantey served under Stonewall Jackson until he was commissioned a general.

> John D. Kennedy, although wounded several times, recovered to be promoted to his command at the age of twenty-four.

> Zack C. Deas, who, with $28,000 worth of his own gold, purchased rifles for his men and led them to Shiloh.

CONFEDERATE MONUMENT

Monument Square, Laurens and Broad Streets. The monument here honors the Confederate dead. The inscription reads, "Brave sons who fell during the Confederate War; defending the rights and honor of the South."

Besides sacrificing their sons on distant battlefields, the residents of Camden suffered greatly as a result of a brutal attack in February 1865 by forces of Sherman's army.

KING HAIGLAR WEATHER VANE

Replicas may be seen at the Camden City Hall, 1000 Lyttleton Street, and at the Camden Opera House, 900 Broad Street. King Haiglar, a noble

Catawba Indian chief, insisted on remaining friendly with the colonists during the Cherokee-Catawba wars (1758–1761). A grateful South Carolina Assembly provided the Catawba with food and equipment. In 1763, King Haiglar was killed by members of a hostile tribe.

J. B. Mathieu designed and executed (between 1815 and 1825) this five-foot memorial weather vane, which has always been placed on the highest building in the city. Residents refer to the peace-loving King Haiglar as "the patron saint of Camden."

SPRINGDALE RACE COURSE

200 Knights Hill Road. Phone: (803) 432-6513. Since 1930 the annual Carolina Cup, one of the nation's outstanding horse-racing events, has been held here. The Colonial Cup, an international steeplechase now carrying a purse of $150,000, was first run at this track in 1970.

RECOMMENDED SIDE TRIPS
WINNSBORO

To get to Winnsboro from Camden, travel west on Route 34 for approximately 30 miles.

After the American victory at Kings Mountain (October 7, 1780), Lord Cornwallis led the remnant of his field forces in harried retreat. It had rained for days, and the roads became so muddy that they were practically impassable. Provisions were low and the soldiers grew weak and ill. After fifteen days, they arrived, battered and weary, at Winnsboro.

While the British remained here from October 1780 to June 1781, reinforcements arrived and rebuilt the army's strength to almost 4,000. From here Cornwallis moved on to Charlotte and then toward Yorktown.

BRATTON HOUSE

Bratton and Zion Streets. Not open to the public. Richard Winn, for whom Winnsboro was named, gave this property in 1777 to his daughter Christina, the bride of Colonel William Bratton of York County, who is thought to have fought in several Revolutionary War campaigns.

CORNWALLIS HOUSE

8 Zion Street. Not open to the public. The original section of this house is presumed to have been used by Cornwallis as his headquarters during the occupation of Winnsboro.

FORTUNE SPRINGS GARDEN

Between High, Chalmers, and Park Streets. John Buchanan, a captain in the Continental Army, gave this land to Pompey Fortune, his former slave who had served General Lafayette during the War of Independence. In 1825, Fortune rode to Columbia (about thirty miles away) to pay his respects to Lafayette, who had returned to the United States for a visit.

MOUNT ZION INSTITUTE SITE

Walnut Street between Bratton and Hudson Streets. Not open to the public. Mount Zion Institute was chartered February 13, 1777, by the General Assembly as a public school. The school was closed during the British occupation because the property was used to quarter soldiers. It burned in 1867 but was reconstructed six years later. The former building on this site is believed to be the first public school in the state outside Charleston. A marker recording the institute's history was erected by the Thomas Woodward Chapter of the Daughters of the American Revolution.

NINETY-SIX

Ninety-Six is located near the town of Greenwood. A major battle of the Revolutionary War occurred here in the Southern backcountry.

In mid-May 1781, Patriot General Nathanael Greene began marching 1,000 soldiers toward the village of Ninety-Six, a strategic enemy stronghold in the interior of South Carolina. When the troops arrived in the area on May 22, they immediately began digging entrenchments and erecting defenses in preparation for their siege.

Ninety-Six was heavily fortified: Attached to the high walls that enclosed the village were a star-shaped redoubt (the Star Redoubt) on the east end and a stockaded fort (Fort Holmes) on the west end. Patriot artillery fire was first directed against the Star Redoubt, but it was bravely defended by the Loyalists within. At the suggestion of

Henry ("Light-Horse Harry") Lee, Greene initiated efforts to launch an assault against Fort Holmes, which, if successful, would also cut off the village's water supply.

But before this could be accomplished, the Patriot generals received a dispatch indicating that British reinforcements under Lord Rawdon were marching to relieve the besieged garrison at Ninety-Six. Realizing he must take immediate action, General Greene ordered an all-out attack. On the afternoon of June 18, Lee's detachment stormed Fort Holmes while troops under Lieutenant Colonel Campbell attacked the Star Redoubt. Although Lee's forces were able to fight their way into and take

General Nathanael Greene by Valentine Green (after Peale) (NATIONAL PORTRAIT GALLERY, SMITHSONIAN INSTITUTION)

possession of the fort, Campbell's men were driven back during their attempt to penetrate the abatis surrounding the redoubt.

With nearly 130 Patriot casualties and with Rawdon's forces swiftly approaching, Greene ordered a general retreat on June 19.

NINETY-SIX BATTLEFIELD SITE
1103 Route 248.

VISITOR INFORMATION A visitor center, maintained by the National Park Service, includes a small museum containing artifacts found at the site. A video explains battles in the area and other local historical events. Open Wednesday through Sunday, 9 a.m. to 4:30 p.m. Hours vary by season. No entrance fee. Many living history reenactments are scheduled throughout the year. Consult the website: nps.gov/nisi/planyourvisit/hours.htm.

Birmingham Monument

James Birmingham is considered the first South Carolinian killed in the Revolutionary War. He was a member of the Long Cane Militia, operating near Long Cane Creek and engaging in skirmishes with British regulars and Loyalists before the Siege of Ninety-Six.

Star Fort

The original earthen (compressed earth) walls were fourteen feet high with sandbags placed along the upper rim. In addition, a formidable abatis of sharpened logs surrounded the exterior perimeter. Henry Haldane, the engineer, insisted that the fort be an eight-point structure, thereby permitting maximum cannon and musket fire in multiple directions. Construction started in 1780 and was completed in early 1781.

Stockade / Fort Holmes

Built of timber and connected by trenches to the larger Star Fort (one-half mile east), this stockade—also known as Fort Holmes for the Loyalist owner of the property—protected the area's crucial water supply. Eventually the fort was abandoned and fell into disrepair; visitors now view a reconstruction.

Lancaster

WAXHAWS—REVOLUTIONARY WAR HISTORY

The Battle of Waxhaws (also known as Buford's Massacre) on May 29, 1780, was a devastating defeat for the Patriots.

Near the North Carolina–South Carolina border, British Colonel Banastre Tarleton, with a force of 149 cavalry and infantry, confronted a detachment of approximately 420 Patriot troops led by Colonel Abraham Buford. Tarleton, confident of victory, sent an offer to surrender, which Buford quickly rejected. Soon afterward, British and Loyalist troops charged. Overwhelmed, some of Buford's men attempted to surrender, but they were savagely attacked—113 killed, 150 wounded, and dozens captured. British casualties were light—5 killed and 12 wounded.

This military engagement evolved into a propaganda strategy to incite resentment against the British and increase Patriot recruitment. Because Tarleton's men shot at surrendering combatants, showed no leniency, and refused to take and humanely treat prisoners—"no quarter" in military terms—it signaled a brutal approach that profoundly influenced the colonists. Conflicting accounts exist about the Battle of Waxhaws, including one that Tarleton was pinned under his horse. But Patriot soldiers in future battles—especially in the South—would howl "Tartleton's Quarter" and "Remember Buford" while attacking their enemy.

THE BATTLE OF WAXHAWS AND BANASTRE TARTLETON

Twenty-six-year-old Colonel Banastre Tarleton became infamous after the Battle of Waxhaws. A narrative developed throughout the colonies that Tarleton had tricked Buford's soldiers by offering quarter and

Banastre Tarleton by Joshua Reynolds
(THE NATIONAL GALLERY, LONDON)

then massacring them. He established a reputation as an arrogant, defiant, and ruthless man who frequently boasted that he had butchered more men and lain with more women than anyone else in the British army.

Born in Liverpool, England, he quickly rose to the rank of lieutenant colonel and was offered command of the "British Legion" in the colonies in the spring of 1780. He participated in the Battles of Brandywine, Philadelphia, Camden, Cowpens, and Guilford Courthouse, as well as the Siege of Charleston. Among Tarleton's greatest military successes were Moncks Corner / Charleston and Camden. His greatest failure was at Cowpens, South Carolina, with a crushing defeat that not only was a significant personal humiliation but also weakened the British efforts to dominate the South.

After the Revolutionary War, Tarleton returned to England in 1781 and pursued a dual career in politics and the military. He was a member of Parliament for twenty years while continuing to serve in the British army. Promoted to major general in 1794, he held a military command in Ireland and England. He passed away on January 16, 1833.

WAXHAWS BATTLEFIELD SITE

Located at 262 Rocky River Road, 9 miles east of downtown Lancaster, South Carolina (near the North Carolina border). Accessible from Route 521. Open daylight hours. Free. Audio tours are available. This site is administered by the South Carolina Battleground Preservation Trust and the American Battlefield Trust. Phone: (800) 298-7878.

BATTLE MONUMENT (1860)

A ten-foot obelisk marks the mass grave of Patriot soldiers. After the Battle of Waxhaws, local farmers were ordered to bury the dead at this site. Wounded soldiers were carried to the Waxhaws Presbyterian Church, but many died and then were buried nearby.

BATTLE MONUMENT (1955) / "THE SECOND MONUMENT"

A second, newer monument was erected here ninety-five years after the first one because the original monument was severely damaged by souvenir seekers, who chipped away at the stone.

DAR MARKERS

Daughters of the American Revolution placed (in 1965 and 2005) memorial markers honoring the fallen warriors.

INTERPRETATIVE SIGNS

Placards provide relevant information about local military history.

NON-REVOLUTIONARY SITES OF INTEREST

ANDREW JACKSON STATE PARK

196 Andrew Jackson Park Road. Located approximately 9 miles north of Lancaster on US 521. Open daily November 1 through March 31, 8 a.m. to 6 p.m.; April 1 through October 31, 9 a.m. to 9 p.m. Adults $3, children $1. Information available at the museum (see below). Phone: (503) 285-3344.

Born in the Waxhaws region, Andrew Jackson (1767–1845) supported the Patriot cause during the Revolutionary War. As a young courier, he was captured by the British and endured brutal treatment. He later served as a congressman and senator, representing Tennessee. He gained fame for his military leadership at the Battle of New Orleans during the War of 1812. Elected the seventh US president, Jackson was inaugurated on March 4, 1829, and served two terms (until 1837). He is buried at "The Hermitage," his plantation near Nashville, Tennessee.

DAR Birthplace Marker

This marker recognizes Andrew Jackson's birthplace in this area (although North Carolina also claims his birthplace).

Museum

Usually open Saturday and Sunday, 1 p.m. to 5 p.m. Hours vary by season. The museum also functions as an information center; tours are available. The museum offers exhibits highlighting President Jackson's achievements and showing a collection of Revolutionary War artifacts. Especially fascinating are the displays about the life and culture of the South Carolina backcountry.

Recreation Areas

Hiking and biking trails, picnic shelters, and campsites are available. Check hours and safety regulations.

Replica of Schoolhouse

Hours vary by season. A fine replica of an eighteenth-century schoolhouse re-creates the environment where backcountry children received basic education.

Statue of Jackson

This bronze statue of the young Andrew Jackson was created by prominent sculptor Anna Hyatt Huntington (1876–1973) and dedicated in 1967.

NATIVE AMERICAN STUDIES CENTER AT USCL

119 South Main Street. Usually open Tuesday and Wednesday, 10 a.m. to 5 p.m.; Thursday, 10 a.m. to 7 p.m. Hours vary. Call (803) 313-7172 to verify hours or to request an appointment.

This center—at the University of South Carolina Lancaster—houses a remarkable collection of Catawba artifacts, pottery, documents, art, and other items related to Native American history and culture. Much of the collection has been transferred to digital format for the archives.

A Catawba reservation is located in Rock Hill, approximately twenty miles from this campus. During the Revolutionary War, the Catawba nation in South Carolina allied with the Patriots and fought against the British and Loyalists, who burned their villages in retaliation. Catawba men were fierce warriors and served as invaluable scouts and guides because of their knowledge of the terrain.

Spartanburg Area

KINGS MOUNTAIN—REVOLUTIONARY WAR HISTORY

In late 1780, after Gates's disaster at Camden, South Carolina was virtually the undisputed possession of General Cornwallis's army. Major Patrick Ferguson, commanding a force composed solely of Loyalists, was charged with patrolling the northern part of the colony to inspire local sympathizers to join the British forces. He was then instructed to meet Cornwallis at Charlotte, North Carolina. As Ferguson was moving his army toward Charlotte, the frontiersmen from settlements west of the Blue Ridge Mountains (in present-day Tennessee, North Carolina, and South Carolina) were organizing forces to crush the British-Loyalist presence. Colonel Isaac Shelby and Colonel John Sevier, both respected Patriot leaders, issued an urgent call for volunteers to rally at Sycamore Shoals (near modern Elizabethton, Tennessee). More than 1,000 men responded. On the morning of September 26, 1780, they began their march over the mountains in pursuit of Ferguson's army. Moving southward through North Carolina, they were joined by a continuous stream of volunteers. Finally, the determined frontiersmen reached Kings Mountain (just south of the present-day North Carolina border), where Ferguson's camp of 1,100 men was located on a tapering ridge 500 yards long and raised around 60 feet above the surrounding countryside.

In mid-afternoon on Saturday, October 7, 1780, the major Patriot leaders (Shelby, Sevier, Campbell, Williams, McDowell, Winston, and Chronicle) instructed their detachments to encircle the base of the ridge and then close in gradually from all sides. As the Patriots steadily ascended—moving from boulder to boulder, tree to tree—the Loyalists began to fire incessantly at them. A Loyalist bayonet charge succeeded in repulsing two of the Patriot units, but not for long. Finally, Campbell's and Shelby's men captured the southwestern section of the ridge, and Sevier's corps reached the summit. Within minutes Ferguson's forces were completely surrounded. Terrified, they made a last desperate stand. At the height of the fray, Ferguson was mortally wounded. Shot from his horse and with one foot caught in a stirrup, he was dragged along the battlefield to the Patriot side. After his horse was restrained, his body was stripped and buried in a shallow grave.

An order to surrender was shouted by Captain Abraham de Peyster, who had assumed command. But many Patriots, wishing to avenge relatives and friends killed by the enemy, continued to fire. When order was restored, the victorious frontiersmen collected the prisoners' arms and counted the dead.

While the Patriots lost only twenty-eight men, not one of the Loyalists escaped death or capture. It is noteworthy that with the exception of Major Ferguson, the British forces were composed of colonists. Here, in 1780, South Carolina saw neighbor fighting neighbor and brother fighting brother.

The Battle of Kings Mountain was the turning point of the Southern campaign, the beginning of a series of Patriot victories that ended with the British being driven from the Carolinas.

KINGS MOUNTAIN NATIONAL MILITARY PARK

2625 Park Road near Blacksburg. Open daily 9 a.m. to 5 p.m. Free. Phone: (864) 936-7921. The Kings Mountain Battlefield site is now a military park (administered by the National Park Service) that adjoins Kings Mountain State Park, where swimming, camping, and picnicking are permitted.

VISITOR INFORMATION An information center and museum at the battlefield site houses a diorama of the battle, an electronic map showing the deployment of troops, and a reproduction of a rare breech-loading rifle, invented by Patrick Ferguson. The building is open Wednesday through Sunday, 9 a.m. to 5 p.m. Closed Martin Luther King Jr. Day, Washington's Birthday, Labor Day, Columbus Day, Veterans Day, Thanksgiving, December 25, and January 1. Free. From here, visitors may follow a foot trail that leads to the major points of interest. Self-guided audio tours are available.

CENTENNIAL MONUMENT

Erected in 1880 in memory of the American Patriots who defeated Ferguson, this monument is placed on the highest peak of the battle ridge—where the men under Shelby, Campbell, and Sevier overpowered the Loyalists.

THE CHRONICLE MARKERS

When his troops wavered, Major William Chronicle urged them on, shouting, "Face to the hill!" They moved ahead even as he was struck and killed. Legend has it that he was buried wearing the ring presented to him by his fiancée, Margaret Alexander.

The marker to the left is the original stone erected in 1815 by Dr. William McLean, surgeon to the Patriot forces that participated in the battle. It marks the grave of the twenty-five-year-old Major Chronicle, a North Carolina officer, who is buried here alongside Captain John Mattocks, John Boyd, and William Rabb. In 1914, the Kings Mountain Association of York, South Carolina, erected the second marker, which stands to the right. The DAR replaced the original weather-beaten marker in 1930.

FERGUSON'S GRAVE

Born in Aberdeenshire, Scotland, Patrick Ferguson received his military training at an academy in London. He entered the British army in July 1759 and, after seeing service in Flanders and Germany, was sent to America in 1777. He fought at Brandywine and Charleston before he was assigned to organize and train the Loyalist militia in South Carolina.

His outstanding contribution to the science of weaponry was the development of the first breech-loading rifle to be used by troops in battle. Known as the Ferguson Rifle, it was effective for its rapid-firing capabilities, which surpassed those of the front-loading muskets of the period. The rifle was first used in the Battle of Brandywine (September 11, 1777) by troops trained by Ferguson. The large tablet marking Ferguson's grave was dedicated October 7, 1930, by President Herbert Hoover on the occasion of the Sesquicentennial Celebration of the Battle of Kings Mountain. The headstone is seven feet high and two feet

Ferguson's Grave, Kings Mountain (NATIONAL PARK SERVICE)

wide, with a finely bordered oval circle bearing the inscription *"Dieu et mon droit"* (God and my right) and *"Honi soit qui mal y pense"* (Evil to him who evil thinks)—the respective mottoes of the British Royal Arms and the Order of the Garter.

Following the Scottish custom, visitors have placed stones on Ferguson's grave to prevent his spirit from wandering. Over the years the mound of rocks has grown steadily.

HAMBRIGHT MONUMENT

Erected by the DAR, this monument marks the location where Patriot leader Colonel Frederick Hambright (1727–1817) was wounded during the battle. Serving as a member of the North Carolina Provincial Congress, he joined the Revolutionary War in 1777 with the rank of lieutenant colonel in the Lincoln County Regiment. He was commended for his bravery by the North Carolina General Assembly after suffering a serious wound at Kings Mountain.

UNITED STATES OBELISK

Congress authorized $30,000 for the erection of this monument, which was completed in 1909. Designed by the prestigious firm McKim, Mead and White, the eighty-three-foot white marble obelisk was dedicated before dignitaries from the major Southern states. On the east side of the obelisk is a plaque listing the names of the Patriots who died in the Battle of Kings Mountain. On the west side a plaque names the officers serving here.

COWPENS—REVOLUTIONARY WAR HISTORY

In late fall 1780, after General Gates's disastrous retreat from Camden, the Continental Congress appointed General Nathanael Greene commander of the Southern forces. In December, Greene arrived at Charlotte, North Carolina, where the bruised Americans had been preparing to encamp for the winter.

While bivouacked at Charlotte under Gates, the Americans had so pillaged the countryside for provisions that little more could be obtained, and local inhabitants were becoming increasingly hostile to the Patriot cause. Greene decided to remove his forces to South Carolina, where they could repair their equipment and regain their strength. Against orthodox military strategy, he split his already meager forces and placed a unit of the men under Colonel Daniel Morgan with the intention of diverting the British from the Patriots' southward movement. As Morgan marched toward the British, his ranks were swelled by groups of militia.

The Battle of Cowpens—Conflict between Colonels William Washington and Banastre Tarleton, engraving after A. Chappel (UNIVERSITY OF SOUTH CAROLINA)

In early January 1781, General Cornwallis, fearing that Morgan would interfere with his plans to march northward toward Virginia, dispatched roughly 1,000 soldiers under Lieutenant Colonel Banastre Tarleton to drive Morgan's troops from the area. On January 17, the opposing forces met in South Carolina at Cowpens (so called because it was the spot where local farmers gathered their cattle before sending them to market).

Morgan devised a shrewd deployment of forces for the coming confrontation. He formed three parallel lines of his men approximately 150 yards apart. The first and second lines, composed of unseasoned militiamen, were ordered to fire only two volleys and then fall back behind the third line. Hidden behind a ridge, the third line of experienced soldiers, eager for battle, fired ferociously at the oncoming enemy. Nearby, Colonel William Washington's cavalry waited in reserve.

Tarleton, mistaking this maneuver for a retreat, ordered his infantry and dragoons to advance. To their surprise, the third American line held fast and fought aggressively. Shooting low, they fired round after round, but the equally courageous Redcoats continued to attack. Simultaneously, Washington's cavalry circled around, striking the British from the rear. Seeing the disorder in the British ranks, the Americans charged with their bayonets. At a call to surrender, the Redcoats threw down their arms; some fled in panic.

William Washington's horsemen followed the fleeing British cavalry, and at one point the two officers crossed swords, engaging in a personal duel. Tarleton managed to fire his pistol at his adversary and escape, but the bullet wounded Washington's horse instead. As another British officer thrust forward to kill Washington, his young bugler shot that officer and saved Washington's life.

Although the opposing forces were virtually equal in number, Morgan's leadership won the day. In preparing his battle formation, he had carefully assessed the abilities of his men and devised a strategy that minimized their inexperience. The Battle of Cowpens was a decisive victory for the Americans—no British were killed, but more than 800 were captured; only 12 Americans were lost.

COWPENS NATIONAL BATTLEFIELD SITE

4001 Chesnee Highway, Gaffney. Open daily, 9 a.m. to 5 p.m. Hours vary by season. Closed major holidays. Free. Phone: (864) 461-2828.

BATTLE MONUMENT / WASHINGTON LIGHT INFANTRY MONUMENT

In 1856, the Washington Light Infantry Brigade of Charleston made a pilgrimage to Cowpens to erect a commemorative stone on the spot where Colonel William Washington's troops had taken their stand.

They were cordially welcomed on their arrival in Spartanburg (then a town of about 2,000 inhabitants) on Saturday, April 19, and spent the weekend as guests of the townspeople. Early Monday morning, the men of the Washington Light Infantry, bearing the standard carried by Colonel William Washington's regiment seventy-five years earlier, journeyed to the Cowpens Battlefield site.

The day was spent in erecting a monument—a fluted iron shaft topped by a bronze eagle set on an octagonal marble slab base. The following day (April 22), at noon, a gala dedication was held with speeches, military drills, lively music, and picnicking. This original monument was destroyed by vandals.

In 1931, the sesquicentennial of the Battle of Cowpens led to plans for a second monument. By this time, the section of Spartanburg County in which the battlefield lay had been taken for the formation (in 1898) of Cherokee County, with its courthouse at Gaffney. The Daughters of the American Revolution of Gaffney raised $1,000 and bought an acre of the battlefield area for the purpose of erecting a second monument a few hundred yards from the Washington Light Infantry shaft. The next year the impressive monument was dedicated with appropriate pomp and ceremony.

In 1980, the golden eagle on top of the original monument was stolen during restoration. It has never been replaced.

INFORMATIONAL SIGNS

Numerous informational signs throughout the battlefield explain military strategies and troop movements.

DOWNTOWN SPARTANBURG

MORGAN STATUE

Intersection of Main and Magnolia Streets. Under the joint auspices of the Washington Light Infantry and a committee of citizens of Spartanburg, the Centennial of the Battle of Cowpens was celebrated by the erection in Spartanburg's public square of a stately column surmounted by a statue of General Daniel Morgan (1736–1802).

In the spring of 1881, large blocks of stone were brought to Spartanburg to form the base and shaft of the monument. After the foundation was in place, the bronze statue (sculpted by J. Q. A. Ward) arrived and was hoisted to the top of the Doric column. The statue represents Morgan in frontier garb; a powder horn is slung over his left shoulder, and in his right hand he holds a sword. (It is believed that the likeness is based on a sketch by artist John Trumbull.)

On May 11, 1881, a cannon salute inaugurated the dedication festivities. Bands blared martial music, flags fluttered gaily in the breeze, and brigades of soldiers marched to the square. Next, eight young ladies—escorted by officers of the Washington Light Infantry—prepared to unveil the statue. In response to a signal, they pulled cords attached to the bunting covering the monument, and the striking statue was seen outlined against the blue sky. Afterward, the assembled crowd listened to speeches by distinguished politicians, including Governor Hagood. Senator Hampton conveyed a message from President James A. Garfield.

General Daniel Morgan, artist unknown (NATIONAL PORTRAIT GALLERY, SMITHSONIAN INSTITUTION)

SEAY HOUSE

106 Darby Road. Open March through November, the second Saturday, 11 a.m. to 4 p.m. Closed major holidays. Adults $8, children (under 5) free, youth (6–17) $5.

The oldest house in Spartanburg, this one-story log structure was once owned by Jammie Seay, a Revolutionary War soldier in the Second Virginia Infantry. Later, in the 1880s, it was occupied by three unmarried sisters. Tour guides highlight not only Revolutionary War history but also how women contributed to the domestic and economic stability of the community. This house is listed in the National Register of Historic Places.

RECOMMENDED SIDE TRIP
WALNUT GROVE PLANTATION

Walnut Grove Plantation is located at 1200 Otts Shoals Road in Roebuck. Open September to May, Thursday through Saturday, 10 a.m. to 5 p.m.; Sunday, 12 p.m. to 5 p.m. Adults $10, children (under 4) free, youth (5–16) $8, active military free. Self-guided tours $5, children (under 3) free, active military free, members free. Closed Easter, Independence Day, Thanksgiving, December 24, December 25, December 31, and January 1.

Walnut Grove Plantation was the home of Charles and Mary Moore, who had first settled in Pennsylvania and then migrated to South Carolina in the early 1760s. After traveling down the Great Wagon Road through Virginia and North Carolina, they finally arrived here, in a land that was wilderness. They hewed down the great walnut and oak trees and, in 1765, built this sturdy Georgian-style structure.

This house is furnished with many fine period pieces, which have been chosen with great care. In front of the **Living Room** fireplace, with its Queen Anne–style mantel, stands a fine eighteenth-century gaming table set up for a game of draughts (similar to checkers). Behind the handsome Chippendale sofa is a chest on which may be seen a 1675 Bible box brought by the Moores to South Carolina. The prints of plants and birds gracing the walls were executed by Alexander Wilson, an artist who traveled throughout the Carolinas in the early 1800s. A family memento on display is the diploma of one of Thomas Moore's sons, Dr. Andrew Moore, who graduated from Dickinson College in 1795, studied with Dr. Benjamin Rush in Philadelphia, and returned to South Carolina to practice medicine.

The **Dining Room**, a post-Revolutionary addition, contains a fine drop-leaf dining table, a Hepplewhite sideboard, a sugar chest, and serving pieces of pewter and delft.

Among the important furnishings in the **Master Bedroom** are a four-poster bed (made in Charleston), a tape loom (used for making narrow tapes or ties), and a trunk (made of European "deal" wood, similar to pine). The portrait above the mantel is of Kate Moore Barry, who served as a spy and courier during the War of Independence. She is said to have gathered valuable information for Colonel Daniel Morgan as he was preparing to confront the British at Cowpens. An excellent horsewoman, she rode through the countryside warning the local Patriots of the British presence.

The large upstairs room was used as a **Bedroom-Dormitory** by the Moore children. Today it is filled with games, dolls, and beds similar to those the youngsters might have used. The partition that separates the small rooms to the side is a later addition. The older children, who needed more privacy, slept here. **Kate's Bedroom** is furnished with a blue-painted Queen Anne bed and a matching blanket chest.

In this upstairs room, Captain Steadman, an officer in the Colonial forces and a friend of the Moores, recuperated from a serious illness. Two fellow soldiers were visiting when word arrived that "Bloody Bill" Cunningham—a Loyalist notorious for his terrorism of the local community—was on his way to wreak vengeance on Steadman for the execution of one of his friends. As Cunningham and a gang approached the Moore house, their raucous shouts unintentionally served as a warning. Steadman's two visitors fled through the back door in an attempt to seek aid but were cut down before they could make their escape. "Bloody Bill" bounded up the stairs and bayoneted the bedridden Captain Steadman.

The house, which is steeped in history, may still contain one of its Revolutionary inhabitants. On several occasions a ghost is reported to have been sighted. Some observers claim that this spectral creature is a woman (perhaps Kate Moore Barry?); others believe it is Captain Steadman in his nightshirt.

The outbuildings on the grounds of Walnut Grove Plantation include:

A **Kitchen** where the food was prepared and other chores performed, such as making candles, preparing dyes, and spinning flax.

A **Blacksmith Forge** where horseshoes, locks, nails, andirons, skewers, and trivets were made.

The **Well House** with a dry cellar in which dairy products, kept in covered crocks and jugs, were stored.

The **Meat House** where meats were smoked and salted.

The **Academy**, a one-room schoolhouse, the first in Up Country South Carolina. Charles Moore was the first schoolmaster here.

Several hundred yards from the house and outbuildings is the **Cemetery** where members of the Moore family, including Kate Barry, are buried. The graves of Captain Steadman and his two companions are also located here.

NORTH CAROLINA

Greensboro Area

GUILFORD COURTHOUSE—REVOLUTIONARY WAR HISTORY

In February 1781, Charles Cornwallis had sent Nathanael Greene's Patriot forces retreating to safety in Virginia. While the British seemed momentarily to have gained the advantage, their provisions were low and the soldiers were weary from their effort to overtake the Americans.

In Virginia, the Patriots' numbers were increased by the local militia, and Greene decided to return to North Carolina to cut off Cornwallis's supply lines and, by his presence in the colony, discourage Carolina Loyalists from joining the British.

Throughout the beginning of March, Greene managed to harass the British while avoiding a direct conflict. By mid-March he had assembled around 4,400 men. Although unsure of their effectiveness in battle, he decided that he would have to confront Cornwallis before the militiamen became discouraged and drifted back to their homes.

On March 15, 1781, Greene waited near Guilford Courthouse for the arrival of Cornwallis. As the Redcoats approached from the west, Greene deployed his troops into three lines and then opened cannon fire. The British quickly brought a gun forward and returned fire while they drew into battle formation.

The British soon attacked the American first line. (Composed mostly of newly recruited North Carolina militiamen, they—like Morgan's first line at Cowpens—were expected to fire two rounds and fall back.) As the Redcoats stubbornly pushed forward until they reached the position of the first line, they suffered heavy casualties.

Then they proceeded toward the American second line (composed primarily of Virginia militiamen). These inexperienced Patriots, no match for the well-trained British, were driven back. The British advanced 400 yards to the American third line. At the sight of the onrushing scarlet-coated soldiers, one of the unseasoned regiments of the third line turned in retreat. But the First Maryland Regulars stood firm; they discharged a volley and sprang forward in a bayonet charge. At that moment, the cavalry of Colonel William Washington swooped down from a nearby hill to join in the fray. The soldiers were engaging in fierce hand-to-hand fighting when Cornwallis, in a desperate maneuver to save the remnant of his battalion of Guards, ordered his cannon to fire "grapeshot" into the melee, even though it would endanger his own men.

The tactic was effective. The British troops regrouped and charged again. Greene, realizing he would have to sacrifice too many of his men to counter another assault, ordered a general retreat. Only after the other regiments had withdrawn did Greene's unit quit the field.

Although the day's victory went to Cornwallis, it was purchased at a high price. More than a quarter of his army had fallen, and the endurance of the British soldiers had been sorely tried.

With his nearest source of food 200 miles away at Wilmington, no foraging party could be safely dispatched into the surrounding countryside, nor could the safety of provisions sent from Wilmington be guaranteed. Cornwallis's forces had been so demoralized that he would have to avoid another major battle—should he sustain substantial losses, his army would be prey to the hostile militia. Subsequently he decided that if Britain was to hold the South, the only hope lay in his pushing north to Virginia and consolidating his forces with those of General Phillips.

GUILFORD COURTHOUSE NATIONAL MILITARY PARK

2332 New Garden Road. Open daily, 8:30 a.m. to 5 p.m. Closed Thanksgiving, Christmas Day, New Year's Day. Free.

The development of the Guilford Courthouse Battleground site was the inspiration of Judge David Schenck of Greensboro, who in October 1886 purchased thirty acres of the land here. During the next thirty years, additional land was acquired and numerous monuments were erected. In 1917, federal legislation created the Guilford Courthouse National Military Park, and since 1933 it has been administered by the National Park Service.

Battle of Guilford Courthouse by H. Charles McBarron Jr. (US CENTER FOR MILITARY HISTORY)

VISITOR INFORMATION Open Wednesday through Sunday, 9 a.m to 5 p.m. Hours vary by season. Closed major holidays. This building houses a small museum with dioramas and Revolutionary War rel cs. A film describes the battle.

To see the major points of interest, visitors to the area may either walk along the footpaths or drive their vehicle down the roads. Many monuments stand proudly on this battlefield site, but the following are highly recommended.

Driving Tour

Start at the Turner Monument, around half a mile before the visitor center.
Turner Monument
Signers Monument / Hooper-Penn Graves
Greene Monument
Maryland Monument
Delaware Monument
Third Line Monument
Stuart Monument
Francisco Monument / Cavalry Monument
Winston Monument
Winston-Franklin Graves
End at the traffic circle near the graves of Winston and Franklin.

DELAWARE MONUMENT

In July 1888, Judge David Schenck, founder of the Guilford Courthouse Battle Ground Company, was searching the battlefield for mementos when he noticed bones protruding from the ground near a small gully. He excavated the area, finding the remains of three men and buttons identifying them as Continental soldiers of Captain Robert Kirkwood's Delaware command. The bones were reinterred at the intersection of Bruce and New Garden Roads, and a marker was erected on the spot. Soon afterward, a shaft of marble was added. The dedication took place in 1892.

FRANCISCO MONUMENT / CAVALRY MONUMENT

On the hill opposite the Third Line Monument stands a cenotaph to Peter Francisco (1760–1836), the seven-foot-tall soldier who was a member of Colonel William Washington's cavalry, which charged the British Guards in the vale below.

Francisco spent his childhood in Virginia. Shortly after the outbreak of the Revolutionary War, he joined the Colonial army and fought in many battles. He is said to have removed a 1,100-pound cannon during the Battle of Camden. According to legend, Francisco, wielding an oversized sword, ferociously slew eleven men in the Battle of Guilford Courthouse before he was critically wounded. He lay close to death on the battlefield for hours before being discovered by a local farmer, who nursed him back to health.

The octagonal shaft—with alternating rough and dressed sections—was erected around 1909 by Peter Francisco Pescud, a descendant of the hero. The monument also serves to commemorate the contribution of the Marquis de Brétigny (a Frenchman who came to America to fight

Francisco Monument, Guilford Courthouse National Military Park (NATIONAL PARK SERVICE)

for the Patriot cause) at the Battle of Guilford Courthouse. Leading a company of North Carolina cavalrymen, he participated in the charge of Colonel William Washington.

GREENE MONUMENT

Directly opposite the Visitor Center—on the ground where the Virginia militia of the American second line took their stand—is the impressive statue of Nathanael Greene. Born in Warwick, Rhode Island, Nathanael Greene (1742–1786) became active in Colonial politics and served in the Rhode Island Assembly (1770–1772, 1775). At the beginning of the American Revolution, he commanded a detachment of militia at the siege of Boston and was in charge of the city after the British evacuation (1776). He fought with Washington (1776–1777) at Trenton, Brandywine, Germantown, and Valley Forge. After Gates was defeated at Camden, Greene was given command of the Southern forces.

Nathanael Greene Monument, Guilford Courthouse National Military Park (ALPER)

On the monument base (white granite on a concrete foundation with a granite trim) stands a ten-foot-high pedestal topped with a bronze equestrian statue (fifteen feet, nine inches high). At center front is a bronze statue of an allegorical figure crowned with a laurel wreath and holding two palm branches in her right hand. In her left hand she holds a shield bearing the emblem of an eagle and thirteen stars.

In 1911, after two decades of determined but unsuccessful efforts by the concerned citizens of North Carolina, Congress passed a bill appropriating $30,000 for a monument to honor Greene. A Commission of Fine Arts was established to supervise a competition for the design of an appropriate statue.

In January 1912, the commission selected a model by Augustus Lukeman. But Paul Schenck, Congressman Charles Steadman, and Senator Lee Overman—a special committee overseeing the project— preferred a model submitted by Francis H. Packer, whose work was finally selected. The preliminary full-size model was approved in 1914 and in the following year was sent to the foundry for casting. Construction of the monument was started in April 1915 and finished only a few days before the dedication ceremonies on July 3.

Another competition was held for the words to be inscribed on the bronze tablet that was to be placed on the front pedestal. The inscription submitted by Dr. C. Alphonso Smith of the University of Virginia was chosen, but the second sentence—with a comment disparaging to the British—was so strongly opposed by the commission and by the secretary of war that it was deleted.

The festive dedication ceremonies were held on July 3, 1915. Before a crowd of thousands, North Carolina dignitaries welcomed the honored speakers: Judge Conrad of the Delaware Supreme Court, Lieutenant Governor Bethea of South Carolina, and Ogden Person, president of the Georgia Senate.

MARYLAND MONUMENT
Soldiers from Maryland played a significant role in the battle. The First and Second Maryland Regiments formed a major portion of Nathanael Greene's third line.

In 1891, the Maryland Historical Society passed a resolution to erect a monument to the memory of the Maryland regiments who fought at Guilford Courthouse. Almost $350 was raised through voluntary contributions, and a granite monument—four feet square and six feet high—was unveiled on October 15, 1892. For the dedication ceremonies, the positions of the Patriot and British regiments during the Battle of Guilford Courthouse were marked by flags. Professor Edward Daves, who had conceived the idea of the monument, delivered the main address.

NO NORTH–NO SOUTH STONE
This small monument has an unusual history. In 1903, the Southern Railway Company had planned to erect a monument to Patriot Calvin Graves but was forced to abandon the project. By this time, however, the stone had been cut and polished. Realizing the face of the stone was too narrow for a full inscription, the members of the Guilford Courthouse Battle Ground Company decided on the following wording:

NO NORTH WASHINGTON

NO SOUTH GREENE

The monument, unveiled July 4, 1904, signifies the common cause that joined North and South during the War of Independence: Washington, a Virginian, commanded Northern troops, and Greene, a Rhode Islander, led the Southern forces.

SIGNERS MONUMENT / HOOPER-PENN GRAVES

This monument honors three North Carolina signers of the Declaration of Independence: Joseph Hewes (1730–1779), John Penn (1741–1788), and William Hooper (1742–1790).

It is interesting to note that none of the three were born in North Carolina. Hewes, a native of New Jersey, settled in Edenton, where he became a successful merchant. He served as a member of North Carolina's Committee of Correspondence and was a delegate to the Continental Congress.

Penn, born in Virginia, moved to Williamsborough, North Carolina, at the age of thirty-three. He was elected to the Continental Congress in 1775.

Boston-born William Hooper settled in the Wilmington area in 1765. He headed the North Carolina delegation to the Continental Congress and later served in the state legislature.

North Carolina Signers of the Declaration of Independence (detail), copy of the Declaration of Independence (THE NATIONAL ARCHIVES, WASHINGTON, DC)

The remains of Hooper and Penn were reinterred here in 1894; Hewes's grave is located in Philadelphia. The bronze figure of Hooper, which was sculpted by A. Pelzer, was dedicated on July 3, 1897.

STUART MONUMENT

Standing near the road in front of the Third Line Monument is the Stuart Monument, which was erected in 1895 on the spot where Colonel Stuart's sword was discovered during excavations.

According to legend, Colonel James Stuart (leader of the Second Battalion of the British Guards) had dueled in January 1781 with Captain John Smith (of Maryland) at the Battle of Cowpens. When the duel proved inconclusive, the two antagonists vowed to fight to the death if they should ever meet again. Two months later, they encountered each other on the Guilford Courthouse battlefield. A fierce hand-to-hand combat ensued, and Colonel Stuart was killed.

THIRD LINE MONUMENT

The tall white column marks the midpoint of the third line, where almost 1,500 American troops resisted the British assault. Little is known about this monument, which was erected in 1910.

TURNER MONUMENT

This bronze statue depicts Mrs. Kerenhappuch Turner. According to tradition, after her son was wounded at the Battle of Guilford Courthouse, she came on horseback from her Maryland home to nurse him back to health. This valiant lady is said to have lived past the age of 100. Several of her descendants became prominent citizens of the South.

The monument was commissioned by Major James Turner Morehead of New York City and was designed by W. H. Mullins of Salem, Ohio. When it was unveiled on July 4, 1902, only the base was in place. The statue was not completed until two months later.

The small triangular marker several yards to the left of the Turner Monument is a memorial to a grandson of Mrs. Turner, James Morehead (1750–1815), who also fought at Guilford Courthouse. The monument, cut in the shape of a small tent, was placed here in September 1900.

WINSTON MONUMENT

The base of this monument was erected on June 6, 1893, as a memorial to the North Carolina troops who fought here under Major Joseph Winston. The next year a statue was commissioned and was mounted during the spring of 1895.

At the age of twenty-three, Virginia-born Joseph Winston moved to North Carolina and settled in Surry County. He served throughout most of the Revolutionary War in the North Carolina Militia. At Guilford Courthouse his troops were almost in constant contact with the Redcoats until Greene ordered the retreat. After the war, Winston served in the state legislature and in the United States Congress. The city of Winston-Salem is named in part for him.

The statue, representing Winston leading a charge of his Surry County Riflemen against Tarleton's Dragoons, was dedicated on July 4, 1895.

WINSTON-FRANKLIN GRAVES

Buried here are Major Joseph Winston (1746–1815) and Captain Jesse Franklin (1760–1823), a member of the Surry County Riflemen and later a US senator and a governor of North Carolina. Their remains were reinterred here in 1906. Nothing is known about Winston's stone; Franklin's stone was removed from the original grave at Fisher's Peak, North Carolina. On July 13, 1966, the Joseph Winston Chapter of the Daughters of the American Revolution of Winston-Salem donated a commemorative plaque to mark the gravesite.

ALAMANCE—REVOLUTIONARY WAR HISTORY

During the decade preceding the formal severing of ties with England, rebellion was stirring in the colonies.

For several years, frontiersmen from the western part of North Carolina had openly opposed the taxes and dishonest officials of the Colonial government. These defiant backwoodsmen became known as "Regulators" because they created disturbances to convince the royal governor that regulation of local officials was necessary.

When in December 1770 the North Carolina Assembly passed the Johnston Riot Act—designed to expedite the arrest and conviction of disturbers of the public peace—the Regulators denounced the repressive act by threatening death to all court clerks and lawyers. They also vowed to assassinate Edmund Fanning, a high-ranking government official whose actions had made him a target of their anger. (He had served as a representative to several Colonial assemblies, was register of deeds of Orange County, and served as a judge of the Superior Court.)

As the unstable conditions continued to prevail, Royal Governor William Tryon prepared a show of force. In early spring, he led the eastern militia, totaling more than 1,000 men, toward Hillsborough and ordered General Hugh Waddell to enlist the support of the western militia and meet him there. Waddell, however, could raise only 200 men. On May 9, Tryon's army reached Hillsborough without incident, but on the same day Waddell's march was halted by 2,000 Regulators,

Royal Governor Tryon and the Regulators, engraving by Albert Bobbett in the book *History of the United States* by Benson Lossing (LIBRARY OF CONGRESS)

87

who blocked his movement at the Yadkin River. Tryon began moving his army westward and on Monday, May 13, encamped on the west bank of Alamance Creek. Remaining there three days, the royal governor tried to negotiate with the Regulators, but no compromise could be reached.

On the morning of May 16, 1771, Tryon's militia marched to within a half mile of the Regulators' camp, and he dispatched a final message ordering the rebels to disperse. When it was rejected, the militia launched a two-hour attack, sending the Regulators fleeing in panic. Eighteen prisoners were taken, along with supplies, ammunition, and seventy horses. Nine Regulators and nine militiamen lay dead on the Alamance battlefield, and many more were wounded.

This show of force by the British added fuel to the spreading fire of Colonial unrest. The Regulator Movement, motivated by local grievances, was a prelude to the expansive conflict of the Revolutionary War—which would erupt in four years' time.

ALAMANCE BATTLEGROUND STATE HISTORIC SITE

5803 Route 62 South. Open Tuesday through Saturday, 9 a.m. to 5 p.m. Hours vary by season. Closed major holidays. Free.

VISITOR INFORMATION An informative film presents details of the Battle of Alamance, and an exhibit describes the Regulator Movement. A small gift shop is open during normal hours.

GUIDED TOURS Guided tours (for a fee) are usually available at 11 a.m., 1 p.m., and 3 p.m., but times vary by season. Tours can be arranged in person or reserved online at www.alamancebattle ground.org/tours.

ALLEN HOUSE

Guided tours available. This small log cabin was moved here from its original location fifteen miles away. It was built by John Allen, who emigrated from Ireland to settle in Pennsylvania. On receiving a land grant in North Carolina from Lord Granville, he traveled to this locale in the late 1750s. Allen's sister Amy married Herman Husband, a leader and pamphleteer of the Regulator Movement. Generations of Allens lived in this house until 1929.

Included among the furnishings, which date from around 1765 to 1825, are a fine tall-case clock, a handsome Chippendale desk, and a walnut blanket chest.

The one-room house also has a loft where the ten Allen children slept. The little porch-room in the rear was used as a general store. The family papers and account books record the sale of items such as herbs, spices, corn, medicines, yarns, cloth, and tools.

BATTLE MONUMENT

This small granite monument, unveiled on May 29, 1880, was given as a memorial to the battleground by Alamance County. The inscription reads, "Here was fought the Battle of Alamance, May 16, 1771, between the British and the Regulators."

HUNTER MONUMENT /
COLONIAL COLUMN

The statue that crowns this monument honors James Hunter, often called the "General of the Regulators." Hunter, a redheaded Scotsman, presented a Regulator petition citing grievances to Royal Governor Tryon at Brunswick Town in June 1768, but Tryon refused to take action. Three years later, during the battle here, Hunter led his valiant men, although in the spirit of brotherhood he proclaimed, "We are all free men and every man must command himself." Following the defeat at Alamance, he escaped to Maryland and went into hiding. While Hunter was in exile,

Hunter Monument, Alamance Battlefield State Historic Site (ALPER)

Tryon placed a sentence of death on him for his part in the rebellion. After the Revolutionary War, Hunter returned to North Carolina and represented the Guilford Courthouse area in the state legislature.

The stone monument base was originally erected on the Guilford Courthouse battleground site in 1901 through donations raised by the Hunter family. Its design is attributed to William C. Noland of Richmond, Virginia. The following year the statue of Hunter (which cost $2,850) was added.

In 1962, the entire monument was transferred to the Alamance battlefield site.

PUGH'S ROCK

According to tradition, James Pugh, one of the Regulators, hid behind this rock during the battle and fired at his enemy. During the height of the fray, he courageously captured one of Tryon's cannon. It was believed that James Pugh was captured and, along with five other Regulators, hanged at Hillsborough, although several historians now believe it was Enoch Pugh (the older brother of James) who was executed.

Winston-Salem (Old Salem)

REVOLUTIONARY WAR HISTORY

The Moravian Brethren are followers of Jan Hus (1369–1415), the Bohemian religious reformer who was condemned as a heretic by the Council of Constance and burned at the stake. In the 1740s, the Moravians established settlements in Pennsylvania, and in 1753 a group of them traveled to North Carolina, where they built a small community named Bethabara (meaning "House of Passage"). Because the town (near present-day Winston-Salem) was primarily engaged in agricultural activity, the Brethren decided in 1766 to build a commercial center on a nearby site. The town, which they named Salem, was carefully planned, street by street. After six years of construction, the first section of houses and shops was completed.

In early 1781, the Revolutionary War reached Salem, bringing with it chaos, fear, and disease. First to arrive were units of General Nathanael Greene's army, which were supplied with provisions. Later, a field hospital was established here briefly; the seriously wounded were left behind to be cared for by one of Salem's physicians, Jacob Bonn.

On February 9, roughly 5,000 Redcoats swarmed the area in pursuit of General Greene's forces. Foraging parties seized livestock and supplies and ripped apart fences and outbuildings to provide wood for campfires. When Cornwallis issued an order for the delivery of twenty horses, many residents hid their horses in the nearby forest.

On February 22, Colonel William Preston and his Patriot soldiers stopped in Salem on their way to Guilford. He ordered none of his men quartered in the houses but asked whether they might be sheltered from the rain in sheds and stables. That evening many of the officers were entertained by a program of organ music, and several of the men spent the night repairing weapons at the blacksmith's forge.

VISITOR INFORMATION

Visit Winston-Salem, 200 Brookstown Avenue; (336) 728-4200. Open Monday through Friday, 8:30 a.m. to 5 p.m.; Saturday, 10 a.m. to 4 p.m. Hours may vary by season. Brochures, maps, and books about the community of Winston-Salem are available here.

Old Salem Museum & Gardens Visitor Center, 900 Old Salem Road; (336) 721-7350. For additional information, visit www.oldsalem .org.

Old Salem, Inc., was organized in 1950 to restore the Moravian settlement founded here in 1766. Buildings erected in the late eighteenth century have been restored or reconstructed, many on the original sites. Visitors should park their vehicles in the lot in front of the visitor center. The major points of interest may be viewed leisurely by walking down Main Street. Walking the area is free, but tickets must be purchased to access the various build-ings, museums, and gardens. Tickets are available at the visitor center or on the website. General admission is usually $20 to $30—higher for special events.

Walking Tour

Start at the Winkler Bakery on South Main Street, just north of Academy Street.

Winkler Bakery

Miksch Tobacco Shop

Wachovia Museum

Single Brothers' House

Vogler House

Salem Tavern Museum

Museum of Early Southern Decorative Arts

End on Main Street near Race Street.

In November 1781, and again in January 1782, the peripatetic North Carolina Assembly met in Salem, but both times it failed to transact business because a quorum was not present.

After the signing in 1783 of the Treaty of Paris—which officially ended the war with England's formal recognition of the independence of the American colonies—the North Carolina Assembly issued a proclamation recommending a statewide observance of the Fourth of July "as a day of Solemn Thanksgiving." The Moravians of this community planned a celebration, believed to be the first such observance by state legislative fiat in America.

On the morning of July 4, 1783, the residents of Salem gathered in the Congregation House to pray, sing hymns, and listen to a sermon delivered by Brother Ludwig Benzien. At 2 p.m., everyone assembled for a "Lovefeast," a simple meal consisting of buns and wine. At dusk a candlelight procession, led by a brass choir, marched singing through the streets.

On the last day of May 1791, President George Washington visited Salem. He spent the day touring the shops, the school, and the waterworks. In the evening he attended a church service, after which he retired for the night to the Salem Tavern.

OLD SALEM SITES
MIKSCH TOBACCO SHOP
532 South Main Street. Owned by the Old Salem Museum and Gardens. When Johann Matthew Miksch built this small house in 1771, he went into business as a bookbinder. Not achieving great success in this endeavor, he opened a tobacco shop, where he sold cut tobacco, chewing tobacco, and snuff. (He was granted permission to do so by the Moravian Church.) Later, he also sold such items as herbs, spices, seed, soap, and small tools. The oldest piece of furniture in this house is the eighteenth-century chest brought here from the Moravian community in Bethlehem, Pennsylvania. Highly prized also is the desk made by John Krauss, a Salem resident. The "perpetual" calendar clock downstairs stopped in 1785.

Bedrooms are located on the second floor.

MUSEUM OF EARLY SOUTHERN DECORATIVE ARTS
924 South Main Street. Open Wednesday through Saturday, 10 a.m. to 4 p.m. Museum-only tickets for adults $15, children (under 3) free, youth (4–17) $15, students $15, members free. Two-stop tickets for adults $22, children (under

3) free, youth (4–17) $10, students $10, members free. All-in-one tickets for adults $30, children (under 3) free, youth (4–17) $16. Closed Thanksgiving, December 24, and December 25. Phone: (336) 721-7360. Opened in 1965, this museum houses a splendid collection of decorative arts and furniture (1660–1820) from various regions of the South. Among the fifteen period rooms, visitors should not miss the elegant Chippendale pieces in the **Edenton Parlor**, the sophisticated decor of the **White Hall Dining Room,** and the finely carved woodwork in the **Edgecombe Room**.

SALEM TAVERN MUSEUM

800 South Main Street. Open Wednesday through Saturday, 10 a.m. to 4 p.m. Adults $30, children (under 3) free, student $16. Phone: (336) 721-7350. The first Salem Tavern, completed in August 1771, was built on the Town Square. The two-story half-timbered building, which measured forty-three feet by thirty-one feet, also had several outbuildings: a kitchen, smokehouse, cow shed, stable, and woodshed.

The first occupants of the tavern were Brother Jacob Meyer, his family, and servants. At first Meyer was paid a salary of £30 a year; later he was permitted to retain a third of his profits as well. His activities were strictly regulated by the laws of the colony and by the Aufscher Collegium. One stricture was that the innkeeper must not allow a guest to become intemperate and run himself into debt. (No one's account could total more than 40 shillings.)

After the devastating fire of January 1784, which destroyed this section of town, another tavern was constructed at a new location. Jacob Meyer and his wife, Dorothea, moved into their second establishment on December 20, 1784, and remained there until 1787, when they retired from the business.

The new tavern keeper was Jacob Blum, who had previously managed the tavern in the nearby community of Bethabara. A justice of the peace, he performed civil wedding ceremonies and collected taxes in Salem.

In the **Gentlemen's Room** of the Salem Tavern—with its Chippendale furniture and fine tablecloths—food was served at any hour. In the **Public Room** across the hall, however, meals were served only at specified hours three times a day.

Food for as many as forty guests was prepared in the large **Kitchen**. The meat and vegetables were cooked in the heavy iron pots hung in the twin fireplaces and were served on pewter platters.

No furniture in the tavern is original except possibly the stretcher table in the **Keeper's Parlor**. The bedrooms are sparsely furnished, and George Washington is said to have spent two nights (in 1791) in the **Blue Room** on the second floor.

SINGLE BROTHERS' HOUSE

600 South Main Street. Owned by the Old Salem Museum and Gardens. This large building housed the unmarried men and older boys of the Moravian community. It was their home and place of business.

The congregation of Salem was divided into groups, or "choirs," according to age, gender, and marital status. Single people lived in one of the Choir Residences—the Single Brothers' House or the Single Sisters'

Single Brothers' House, Old Salem (LIBRARY OF CONGRESS, PRINTS AND PHOTOGRAPHS DIVISION)

House. Married couples lived in their individual homes with their children, who, on reaching the age of fourteen, went to live in the Choir Residences.

After a general education in the Boys' School, the young men came to live here and learned a craft by serving an apprenticeship until they were twenty-one years old.

This structure was built in 1769; in May, scores of workmen gathered for a house-raising bee, and in two days the timbers and rafters were in place. In December, sixteen men and four boys moved in. Seventeen years later, the kitchen was enlarged and additional space for shops was provided.

Visitors can still see in the **Dining Room** the original oak plank floor and the old stove that was used to provide heat. The room is furnished simply, with plain tables and benches. The tables are set with pewter utensils imported from England.

The **Kitchen** is very large and well equipped. The housework was done by the men, and one brother served as a full-time head cook, assisted by young boys. Among the kitchen equipment here is a sifter with a bottom made of horsehair, a lard press, rolling pins, cake pans, and a coffee roaster. The fireplace with its elevated hearth has not been altered. The brick floor is slanted, and an opening appears in the left wall so that dishwater thrown on the floor could be drained out of the building. The southern rooms were used as **Shops**. The tinsmith made household articles such as pots, pans, cookie cutters, candle molds, and even butter churns. The gunsmith crafted fine rifles for hunting, which were sold only to members of the community. In addition, he spent much of his time making door locks, nails, and traps. The joiner's shop—now equipped with two lathes from the shop of Johann Simon Leicht and a workbench from the shop of Henry Leinbach—produced custom-made furniture of walnut, cherry, or maple.

On the second floor is the room of the **Vorsteher**, or supervisor, of the house. The folding bed was raised during the day to create space. The chest of drawers was made locally, and the washstand may be either the original one used here or one from the Single Sisters' House.

Brothers attended services in the **Chapel** on the top floor at least once a day (usually in the evening), when the Scriptures were read and hymns were sung. The organ, which is still in use today, was originally used across the square in the large sanctuary that accommodated the entire congregation. (The benches and brass chandeliers here were also taken from that structure.) The organ was built in Pennsylvania by David Tannenburg, famous maker of musical instruments, and was brought to Salem in 1797. In 2004, it was installed in the Gray Auditorium of the Visitor Center.

VOGLER HOUSE

700 South Main Street. Owned by the Old Salem Museum and Gardens. This house was built in 1819 by thirty-six-year-old John Vogler for his new bride, Christina.

Vogler, who lived to be almost ninety-eight, tried his hand at many occupations. As a young man, he served an apprenticeship to a gunsmith but later decided to become a silversmith. He opened a shop on the ground floor of this house, where he not only sold his silver work but also sold and repaired clocks.

Vogler House, Old Salem (LIBRARY OF CONGRESS, PRINTS AND PHOTOGRAPHS DIVISION)

The French Empire clock here was presented to his daughter when she married in 1838. The profile-making machine standing in a corner was invented by Vogler, who had seen the art practiced in Philadelphia. Cutting silhouettes soon became a lucrative "hobby" for him.

This house was the first in the village to use wallpaper; the paper in the **Family Room** is a reproduction of an eighteenth-century pattern. Articles in the room that belonged to the Vogler family include the ivory chess set, the secretary, and the rocking chair. The paintings above the mantel are of John and Christina Vogler.

Visitors can view some of the original tools Vogler used as well as the old forge that melted the metal for his fine silver objects.

WACHOVIA MUSEUM (BOYS' SCHOOL)

3 East Academy Street. Owned by the Old Salem Museum and Gardens. Phone: (336) 721-7350. This building, constructed in 1794, was used as a boys' school until 1895. The first floor served as the living quarters of the schoolmaster; the classrooms and chapel were located on the second floor; and the students slept in the dormitory on third floor.

Children in colonial costumes playing games, Old Salem (ALPER)

One of the most impressive displays in the museum is the collection of early local pottery by Gottfried Aust and Rudolf Christ. Other important exhibitions include musical instruments (such as harps, dulcimers, tubas, and cornets) and paintings (such as Thomas Sully's *Self Portrait*, Gustavus Grunewald's *Portrait of a Boy*, and Moravian artist John Valentine Haidt's *Queen of Sheba Visiting Solomon*).

The **Annex** houses stagecoaches, a costume and doll collection, and many Native American artifacts.

WINKLER BAKERY

525 South Main Street. Open Wednesday through Saturday, 10 a.m. to 4 p.m. Owned by the Old Salem Museum and Gardens. Phone: (336) 721-7302. John Cristian Winkler was born near Blumenstein, Switzerland, in 1766 and as a young man was apprenticed to a blacksmith. In 1791, he journeyed to Neuwied (Germany) to be received into the Moravian Congregation. Later, he traveled to Ebersdorf, where he learned the baker's trade and was placed in charge of the Brothers' House bakery.

Winkler sailed to America in 1799, was ordained a deacon in Bethlehem (Pennsylvania) in 1802, and finally settled in Salem in 1807, where he purchased this small building for a bakery.

His business flourished. Records indicate he baked almost 200 loaves of bread (in various sizes) in a week. At that time, a five-and-one-half-pound wheat loaf sold for 1 shilling. In addition, rye bread, cakes, and other baked goods were offered for sale.

Hillsborough

REVOLUTIONARY WAR HISTORY

Hillsborough (also spelled Hillsboro) was the scene of the Regulator uprising of 1768. It began when a government official seized a Regulator's horse and saddle for nonpayment of taxes. An outraged band of Regulators rode into town, bound the sheriff, harassed several citizens, and fired shots over the house of Edmund Fanning, one of the royal governor's representatives in the area. Fanning summoned the local militia to search for the leaders of the rioters, and two well-known Regulators, Herman Husband and William Butler, were captured and imprisoned. Enraged by this act, more than 700 Regulators marched into Hillsborough and forced Fanning to free the prisoners on bail. When Husband and Butler were tried at the September term of court, almost 3,000 Regulators encamped on the hills that surrounded the town. Husband was acquitted, but Butler was found guilty.

In September 1770, when the court was hearing a case against several other Regulators, a mob of sympathizers, wielding sticks and cudgels, filled the courtroom. A riot soon erupted. John Williams, an attorney, was severely whipped; William Hooper (later a signer of the Declaration of Independence) was assaulted; and the hated Edmund Fanning was dragged through the streets. Before evening, the mob looted homes and shops and ransacked Fanning's residence.

On June 19, 1771, six Regulators who had fought in the Battle of Alamance (May 16, 1771) were hanged in Hillsborough. Other significant events occurred at Hillsborough: As hostilities with the British intensified and after Royal Governor Martin had fled the colony, a Provincial Congress met here in August 1775, with Samuel Johnston as moderator, and voted to arm two regiments and organize the county militia. The town served as a supply post for Patriot troops and, in 1780, as a rendezvous point for the demoralized army of General Horatio Gates after their defeat at Camden.

Charles Cornwallis occupied Hillsborough for five days in 1781 and raised the royal standard in front of the old courthouse. He tried to induce the young men of the area to join his forces by offering ten days' rations, but few accepted. In September 1781, Hector McNeill and David Fanning, two daring Loyalists, marched with 300 men from British-held Wilmington to Hillsborough and captured Governor Thomas Burke (a native of Hillsborough), several members of his council, and a number of Continental officers. The prisoners were taken back to Wilmington.

Hillsborough was the site of five General Assemblies (1778, 1780, 1782, 1783, and 1784). The state convention, which met here in the summer of 1788, refused to ratify the Federal Constitution. (Every state except North Carolina and Rhode Island had already accepted it.) A second state convention meeting at Fayetteville in November 1789 finally voted to ratify the Constitution.

HILLSBOROUGH SITES
THOMAS BURKE GRAVE
1016 Governor Burke Road. On private property. The tall granite stone here marks the grave of Thomas Burke (1747–1783), member of the Continental Congress (1777–1781) and governor of North Carolina (1781–1782). On September 12, 1781, Burke was captured at his estate, Tyaquin, in a surprise attack by the Loyalists and taken prisoner to Wilmington.

COLONIAL INN
153 West King Street. Since Colonial days, a tavern has stood on this site. The east section was built in 1768. Cornwallis, who made camp in Hillsborough in February 1781, probably visited this tavern. According to tradition, he ordered his soldiers to pave the muddy street here with flat flagstones.

The building is now used as a hotel, and it reopened in 2020 after an extensive renovation.

FANNING HOUSE SITE

Churton Street (Route 70A). A marker indicates the site of Edmund Fanning's house. It is believed that the fine mansion that once stood here was built from money extorted through official fees.

HOOPER HOUSE

118 West Tryon Street. Closed to the public. This home was purchased in 1781 by William Hooper, a signer of the Declaration of Independence, and it was owned by the Hooper family for seventy-two years. When the structure was renovated in the nineteenth century, Hooper's law office, an outbuilding on the northeast corner of the lot, was demolished.

ORANGE COUNTY HISTORICAL MUSEUM

201 North Churton Street. Open daily, 11 a.m. to 4 p.m.; Wednesday by appointment. Free. Phone: (919) 732-2201. This small museum is devoted to eighteenth-century local history. Especially interesting are pieces by early Hillsborough silversmiths, a reproduction of a Colonial kitchen, and a set of standard weights and measures (made in England and purchased by Orange County in 1760).

PRESBYTERIAN CHURCH CEMETERY

Northwest corner of Churton and West Tryon Streets (behind the Presbyterian Church). William Hooper (1742–1790), one of the North Carolina signers of the Declaration of Independence, was buried here before his remains were removed to the Guilford Courthouse battleground site in the early 1920s. But this original grave is still marked by a large stone slab.

The first pastor of the Presbyterian church, Reverend John Knox Witherspoon (1791–1853)—a grandson of John Witherspoon, a New Jersey signer of the Declaration of Independence—is buried in the Nash family plot near the west wall of the cemetery.

REGULATOR MARKER

Corner of East King and Cameron Streets. A bronze marker and a concrete slab indicate the place where six Regulators were hanged on June 19, 1771, after the Battle of Alamance. They were James Pugh (or Enoch

Pugh), Benjamin Merrill, Robert Matear, Robert Messer, and two others whose names have been lost to posterity. The prisoners were escorted to the place of execution by a guard of militiamen.

When they reached the execution site, the condemned men were allowed to speak. Pugh delivered an impassioned defense of the Regulators' cause, and Merrill pleaded for his family's safety. Then they mounted the gibbet, where they were blindfolded and nooses were placed around their necks. As a wail arose from the assembled crowd, they were hanged.

SITE OF TRYON'S MILITARY CAMP

On the banks of the Great Alamance Creek. In May 1771, before proceeding to Alamance to crush Regulator resistance, Governor William Tryon set up a temporary camp in the meadow along the south bank of the Eno River.

Wilmington Area

REVOLUTIONARY WAR HISTORY

When the Stamp Act was passed by the British Parliament in 1765, the people of eastern North Carolina vowed to defy it; large crowds met in Wilmington in open opposition. During the evening of October 31, 1765—the night before the Stamp Act was to take effect—a mob of rowdy demonstrators burned an effigy of "Liberty" to dramatize England's abuse of their rights. Two and a half weeks later, an angry crowd harassed Stamp Master William Houston into resigning his office. These acts of civil disobedience and other spontaneous outbreaks throughout the colonies forced Parliament to repeal the act in the following year. But the injustices against the colonies continued to multiply.

In June 1775, the Patriots of the Wilmington area assembled at the courthouse to proclaim their unity in supporting the acts of the Provincial Council. They passionately declared themselves ready to defend North Carolina even if it meant the sacrifice of their "lives and fortunes to secure her freedom and safety."

In early February 1781, Charles Cornwallis decided to establish Wilmington as a supply base and center for military operations. He dispatched Major James Henry Craig with a battalion of 400 men and a small naval force under Captain John Barclay to capture the city. Their timing was propitious—the bulk of Patriot troops was engaged elsewhere, making the capture of Wilmington an easy victory. On April 7, Cornwallis set up his headquarters in the home of George Burgwin, a leading businessman. The British troops, making forays into the surrounding countryside, plundered farms and homes and captured Patriot leaders.

One evening several Patriots were meeting at the Rouse House, a tavern several miles outside of Wilmington, to play whist and socialize, but the innocent gathering was interpreted as a clandestine political meeting. A squadron of Major Craig's dragoons marched to the inn and slaughtered every man except one, who had concealed himself in a large chimney. The infamous deed has gone down in local history as "The Massacre of the Rouse House."

Cornwallis and the army left Wilmington on April 25, 1781, and marched toward Virginia. A few units under Major Craig, supported by the British warships in the harbor, remained in the town until mid-November 1781—roughly one month after Cornwallis's surrender at Yorktown.

VISITOR INFORMATION

Tourist information and maps of historic Wilmington may be obtained from the **Chamber of Commerce**, 1 Estell Lee Place; (910) 343-0106.

Wilmington, North Carolina, Visitors Booth, 2 South Water Street. Open daily March to May, 9 a.m. to 4:30 p.m.; June to August, 9:30 a.m. to 5 p.m.; September to October, 9 a.m. to 4:30 p.m.; November to February, Friday through Sunday, 10 a.m. to 4 p.m.

Wilmington Convention and Visitors Bureau, 10 Convention Center Drive; (910) 251-5101.

PUBLIC TRANSPORTATION Bus service is provided by Wave Transit, (910) 762-2611 or go to www.wavetransit.com.

TAXI SERVICE Angel's Taxi LLC and Angel's Shuttle Service LLC, (910) 796-8956; Yellow Coastal Cab, (910) 762-4464.

COLONIAL AND REVOLUTIONARY WAR SITES
CORNWALLIS HOUSE / BURGWIN-WRIGHT HOUSE

224 Market Street. Open Monday through Saturday, 10 a.m. to 4 p.m. Adults $20, children (under 5) free, youth (6–17) $10, seniors $18, students $18, members free. Phone: (910) 762-0570. This handsome house was built in 1770–1771 by John Burgwin, formerly treasurer of the colony under Royal Governor Arthur Dobbs. Prior to the signing of the Declaration of Independence, Burgwin was traveling in England and injured his leg, which caused him to extend his stay. When conditions in the colonies worsened, he decided to remain in England until order had been restored.

After Burgwin's departure, the residence was occupied by Judge Joshua Wright and his family, although he did not purchase the property until April 1799.

On April 7, 1781, when Lord Cornwallis arrived in Wilmington after the Battle of Guilford Courthouse, he selected this eight-room,

Cornwallis (Burgwin-Wright) House, Wilmington (LIBRARY OF CONGRESS, PRINTS AND PHOTOGRAPHS DIVISION)

two-story house for his headquarters. The basement was probably used as a prison during the British occupation.

According to legend, one of the Wright daughters was attracted to a young British staff officer, and the couple frequently met under the crab apple tree in the front yard to sip tea and exchange tender glances. To record their affection, the officer engraved their initials on a windowpane.

The house has been restored and furnished with eighteenth-century antiques. Among the notable pieces here are a wing chair from the home of Betty Washington Lewis, a chair from Tryon Palace, a convex mirror owned by Colonel William Washington, a tea table made in Edenton in the 1790s, a Lowestoft punch bowl used by Royal Governor Arthur Dobbs, a 1790 chest of drawers by Philadelphia cabinetmaker Henry Connelly, and a pair of black-and-gold torchères made in England in 1780.

HARNETT MONUMENT

Fourth and Market Streets. This granite shaft was erected by the Colonial Dames of America to honor Cornelius Harnett (1723–1781), a Revolutionary War Patriot who has been called the "Samuel Adams of North Carolina." Harnett served in the Colonial Assembly (1771–1775), accepted the presidency of the Provincial Council of Safety (1776), was a member of the Congress that adopted North Carolina's first constitution (1776), was selected as a delegate to the Continental Congress (1777), and signed the Articles of Confederation (1780).

In the winter of 1781, he was taken prisoner while visiting the home of a friend, Colonel Spicer. Harnett's captors forced him to walk beside the mounted officers as they rode the thirty miles back to Wilmington. When at last he fell exhausted to the ground, they tossed his limp body across a horse and galloped to the town, where he was thrown in prison and died of illness in April. He was buried in the churchyard of St. James.

St. James Episcopal Church, Wilmington
(LIBRARY OF CONGRESS, PRINTS AND PHOTO-GRAPHS DIVISION)

ST. JAMES EPISCOPAL CHURCH

25 South Third Street. Office open Monday through Thursday, 8 a.m. to 4 p.m.; Friday, 8 a.m. to 1 p.m. Phone: (910) 763-1628. St. James Parish, established by an act of the Colonial legislature, was organized in 1729, and the first rector was Reverend John LaPierre. Since construction of the church building was not begun until 1751, members of the parish met for worship in the courthouse.

The first St. James (which had no belfry) was seized by Cornwallis's troops in 1781 and converted into a stable. The present church was erected in 1839.

The painting of Christ titled *Ecce Homo* ("Behold the Man") that hangs here is attributed to the Spanish artist Pacheco (1571–1654). It was taken from a pirate ship that attacked Brunswick Town (fourteen miles away) in 1748, and the North Carolina General Assembly presented it to the parish three years later.

In the churchyard are buried Cornelius Harnett, a Revolutionary War Patriot; Philadelphia-born Thomas Godfrey, author of *The Prince of Parthia* (1767), the first American play performed by a professional company; and Major George W. Glover, the first husband of Mary Baker Eddy, founder of Christian Science.

STAMP ACT DEFIANCE MONUMENT

Fourth and Market Streets. This stone marker tells of the armed resistance in 1765 to the Stamp Act imposed by Parliament. On this spot, the location of the courthouse, a mob forced the stamp master appointed by the Crown to resign his office on November 16, 1765. In June 1775, citizens of New Hanover County assembled here to express their support of the Provincial Congress.

IMPORTANT COLONIAL HOUSES

SITE OF THE HOOPER HOUSE

24 North Second Street. William Hooper, a signer of the Declaration of Independence, lived in Wilmington from 1764 until the close of the Revolutionary War, when he moved to Hillsborough. It is believed that his law offices were located here.

SITE OF THE QUINCE-WASHINGTON HOUSE

Southeast corner of Dock and Front Streets. On Sunday, April 24, 1791, President George Washington visited Wilmington after his tour of New Bern. He was escorted by the Light-Horse Guards (Wilmington's military company), and he entered the town to the thunder of artillery and the cheering of crowds. He occupied rooms at the residence of Mrs. John Quince. The following evening bonfires illuminated the town as a ball was held in the Assembly Hall to honor the distinguished guest. Washington departed on Tuesday, April 26.

NON-REVOLUTIONARY SITES OF INTEREST
DUDLEY MANSION
400 South Front Street. Not open to the public. This was the residence (constructed c. 1830) of the first governor elected by the people of North Carolina, Edward Bishop Dudley (1837). It is now used as the Elks Club.

NATIONAL CEMETERY
2011 Market Street. More than 2,000 Union soldiers, many of whom participated in the 1864 assault on Fort Fisher (around twenty-five miles south of Wilmington), are buried here.

NORTH CAROLINA *BATTLESHIP MEMORIAL*
1 Battleship Road NE. Open daily, 8 a.m. to 5 p.m.; Christmas Day, 12 p.m. to 5 p.m. Adults $14, children (under 5) free, youth (6–11) $6, seniors $10. Phone: (910) 399-9100. Dedicated to the North Carolinians who sacrificed their lives in World War II, this ship is now open to visitors. A museum provides a visual history of the many Pacific campaigns in which the *North Carolina* participated, earning twelve battle stars.

SITE OF ANNA WHISTLER HOUSE
Orange and Fourth Streets, marker at Orange and South Third Streets. The home of the mother of artist James Abbott McNeill Whistler (1834–1903) was once located here. She served as a model for his painting *Arrangement in Black and Gray* (1872), commonly known as *Whistler's Mother.*

BRUNSWICK TOWN—REVOLUTIONARY WAR HISTORY
A thriving port town stood on this site two centuries ago. In 1725, Maurice Moore was granted 1,500 acres of land on the west side of the Cape Fear River. He set aside 320 acres for a community, Brunswick Town. Cornelius Harnett Sr. of Edenton bought the first two lots in June 1726, and after he built his home, he began operating a ferry across the river.

Other houses and shops sprang up, and a small town soon flourished here.

In 1731, Brunswick Town became the official port of entry of the Cape Fear River: All ships entering and leaving were required to secure official approval to pass here.

After the Stamp Act went into effect in 1765, around 450 armed residents of the area marched on Governor Tryon's residence (then located at Brunswick Town). Another angry mob later forced William Pennington, comptroller of customs, to swear under oath that he would not issue stamped paper.

The next year, a British man-of-war seized three merchant ships—the *Dobbs*, the *Patience*, and the *Ruby*—because the papers granting them permission to sail were not properly stamped. The outraged residents of Brunswick Town retaliated by refusing to sell the British much-needed provisions, and a group of several hundred armed men from the lower Cape Fear region finally coerced the British naval officer, Captain Jacob Lobb, into permitting the American ships free access. In the spring of 1776 (following the Loyalist defeat at Moores Creek Bridge), British troops began arriving off Cape Fear. On May 12, Sir Henry Clinton's ships shelled Brunswick Town and a force of more than 900 men came ashore. Although no major engagement was fought, the soldiers pillaged property and sent residents fleeing. The British finally burned the town, leaving it a deserted ruin.

BRUNSWICK TOWN STATE HISTORIC SITE

8884 St. Philip's Road SE, Wilmington. Open Tuesday through Saturday, 9 a.m. to 5 p.m. Closed major holidays. Adults $4, children $1.

VISITOR INFORMATION A video vividly describes the history of Brunswick Town. A map of the historic area and relevant displays are accessible at the visitor center. Phone: (910) 371-6613.

Visitors should follow the foot trail to view major points of interest.

The foundations of several Colonial Brunswick Town buildings have been excavated and are maintained by the state of North Carolina as archaeological exhibits. Reconstruction of the dwellings is not planned at the present time.

SITE OF COURTHOUSE

With the creation of Brunswick County in 1764, a courthouse was built that was used until 1769, when it was destroyed by a hurricane. A partition wall at the east end once divided the official chambers and the public courtroom. The foundation is twenty-five feet square.

SITE OF HEPBURN-REONOLDS HOUSE

Two wealthy merchants, George Reonolds and Charles Hepburn, bought this lot in 1734 for 10 shillings and built a residence and a shop. Even with the expenses of construction, they realized a handsome profit when they sold the property eight years later for £580.

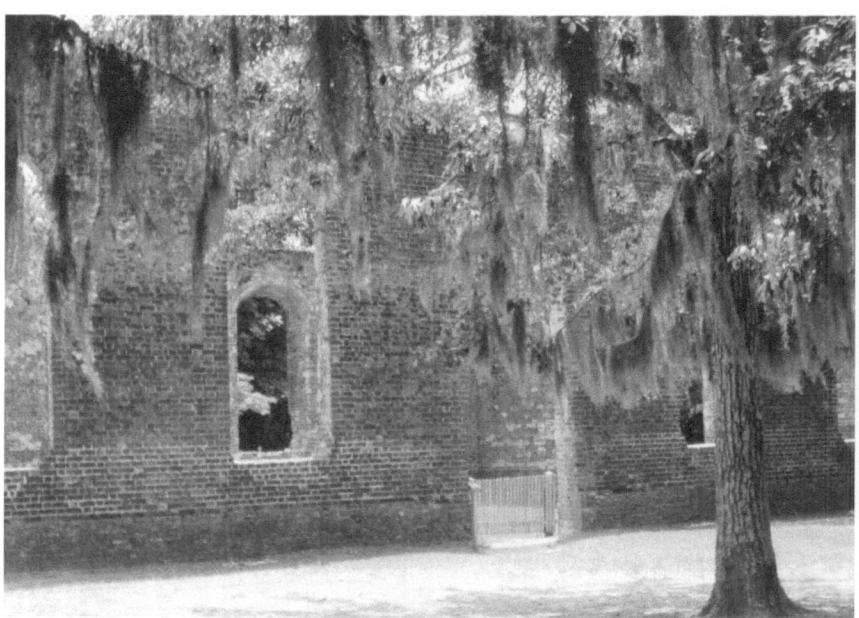

Ruins of a Colonial building, Brunswick Town (ALPER)

SITE OF JOBSON-LEACH HOUSE

This was one of the earliest houses in Brunswick Town. James Leach sold it to the Jobsons of Pennsylvania in 1728. The deed indicates that three years later, James Espry, who owned the adjacent lot, purchased it.

SITE OF WILLIAM LORD HOUSE

The structure once located here may have been a tavern or an inn, as records show that William Lord was a "Tavern Keeper." In his will, dated July 5, 1748, he left his property to a wife and six children.

SITE OF MAURICE MOORE HOUSE

In 1759, Judge Maurice Moore, son of the founder of Brunswick Town, built an impressive house facing Front Street (the road that ran parallel to the river). A porch extended across the entire front of the large structure, and formal gardens graced the grounds.

SITE OF NATHANIEL MOORE HOUSE

Built in the late 1720s, the structure that once stood here had three dormer windows, two brick chimneys on each side of the house, and a porch raised above the ground. Even after Nathaniel Moore sold this river-view property in 1733, it continued to be known as "Nat Moore's Front."

SITE OF ROGER MOORE HOUSE

Colonel Maurice Moore, founder of the town, sold this lot to his brother Roger. Since Roger was residing at nearby Orton Plantation, the house on this site was occupied by tenants.

SITE OF NEWMAN-TAYLOR HOUSE

The two-story brick structure that once stood on this site was built in 1766 by Captain Stephen Newman. Since this house was not burned by the British, it is assumed he was a Loyalist sympathizer. In the late 1770s, the dwelling was purchased for £600 by N. Taylor, who added two rooms (one at the back, the other at the front). The house was torn down around 1800.

SITE OF PUBLIC HOUSE

The Public House was probably a six-room stone structure with a peaked roof, several dormer windows, and three chimneys. A low wall enclosed the grounds of the property. Archaeological evidence indicates that a tailor shop was located in one of the rooms here.

SITE OF RUSSELLBOROUGH

Royal Governor Arthur Dobbs, wishing to improve his health, established a residence in Brunswick Town in 1758; he purchased the large house of Captain John Russell of His Majesty's sloop *Scorpion*. It is evident that the air of Brunswick Town had a salubrious effect on Dobb's health—four years later, the seventy-three-year-old gentleman fell in love and married Justina Davis, a fifteen-year-old resident of the area.

After Dobbs's death in 1765, Royal Governor William Tryon purchased the property. (Construction of the Governor's Palace in New Bern did not begin until 1767.) He changed the name to "Castle Tryon," built a three-room kitchen outbuilding, planted formal gardens, and constructed a tunnel leading from the cellar to the river. Rice was grown in fields along the riverbank northward from the house.

When Governor and Mrs. Tryon moved in 1770 into their luxurious residence in New Bern, William Dry of Brunswick Town became owner of this estate. Although located some distance from the center of the town, Dry's elegant house and furnishings did not escape destruction at the hands of the British in 1776.

WALLS OF ST. PHILIP'S CHURCH

St. Philip's Church was begun in 1754, and construction of the building took fourteen years. Because of the great expense involved, in 1760 the Reverend John McDowell was forced to raise more money to continue work on the structure. With the aid of Richard Quince (a prominent local merchant) and Royal Governor Arthur Dobbs (who wished to make St. Philip's the King's Chapel of North Carolina), sufficient funds were collected. But shortly afterward, construction was further delayed by natural causes—lightning struck the roof, which collapsed. By the time the church was dedicated on May 24, 1768, both McDowell and

Dobbs had died and had been buried here. The original communion plate, surplice, and Bible were gifts of King George III.

Many distinguished colonists worshipped at St. Philip's, including Governor William Tryon, Judge Maurice Moore, Robert Howe, and John Wilkens.

When the British burned Brunswick Town in 1776, this fine church was left in ruins.

ORTON PLANTATION—REVOLUTIONARY WAR HISTORY

9149 Orton Road SE, Winnabow. Orton Plantation is located 2.5 miles from Brunswick Town. Closed to the public. Orton Hall was built in 1725 by "King" Roger Moore, brother of Colonel Maurice Moore, founder of Brunswick Town. Named for the ancestral home of the Moores in England, Orton Plantation was a leading producer of rice. A relative of the Moores, Richard Quince, was the next owner and held possession of the estate for thirty years. The property then passed to Benjamin Smith, who had served as an aide-de-camp to General George Washington and later became a governor of North Carolina. In the early 1840s, Dr. Frederick Hill purchased the estate and enlarged the house with a second story and an attic. He further enhanced the mansion by adding a Greek Revival facade with four imposing columns. During the Civil War, Orton Hall was used as a hospital for Northern troops.

In the early twentieth century, the estate was purchased by the Sprunt family, who added the side wings to Orton Hall and planted the beautiful gardens. In 1983, film producer Frank Capra Jr. selected Orton Plantation as a location for his movie *Firestarter*. An influential friend, Dino De Laurentiis, became enchanted with the area and opened a studio in nearby Wilmington. It resulted in numerous opportunities for film and television productions (including *Dawson's Creek*) at Orton and throughout the area.

In 2010, the property was purchased by Louis Moore Bacon, a direct descendant of Roger Moore, the original eighteenth-century builder of this extraordinary house.

CURRIE (MOORES CREEK)—REVOLUTIONARY WAR HISTORY

The Battle of Moores Creek Bridge was fought on February 27, 1776, between a contingent of Loyalists led by Colonel Donald McDonald and a unit of Patriots organized by Colonel James Moore.

In early 1776, as rebellion was beginning to spread throughout the colonies, Royal Governor Josiah Martin issued a call for subjects loyal to the king to unite and take up arms against the insurrectionists. Donald McDonald raised a force of almost 1,500 Loyalists, most of them Scots.

The Patriots had, at the same time, organized themselves into fighting units, and for around two weeks the two opposing forces managed to avoid each other as they rallied sympathizers to their respective standards. Colonel Moore sent word to Colonel Richard Caswell (commanding nearly 800 Patriots) and Colonel Alexander Lillington (commanding nearly 400 men) to join forces with him at the Moores Creek Bridge.

Through a series of military maneuvers and subterfuges, the Patriots triumphed over their foes. On the night of February 26, Caswell and his men marched to the bridge, abandoning their encampment and leaving the fires smoldering to indicate a hasty retreat. Before sunrise, they removed much of the bridge's log floor and coated the remaining logs with tallow and soap.

At dawn (before Colonel Moore had arrived), the Loyalist forces started to rush across the bridge. Colonel Donald McLeod—who had assumed command from McDonald, who had fallen ill—instructed his followers to maintain their balance by thrusting their swords into the slippery logs. Within a moment, the first wave of men was struck by the volley of musket fire that swept across the bridge. Almost every man—including McLeod—fell dead. Panic gripped the other Loyalists, who dashed to cover in the nearby swamp as Caswell's and Lillington's men pursued them.

Although the entire battle lasted only three minutes, at least thirty Loyalists were killed and hundreds were taken prisoner. Yet only one Patriot, Private John Grady, fell mortally wounded.

MOORES CREEK NATIONAL MILITARY PARK

40 Patriots Hall Drive. The battlefield site is accessible daily, but the Visitor Center is open Tuesday through Saturday, 9 a.m. to 5 p.m. Closed Martin Luther King Jr. Day, Washington's Birthday, Juneteenth, Labor Day, Columbus Day, Thanksgiving, Christmas Day, New Year's Day. Free.

BRIDGE

The Moores Creek Bridge has been reconstructed to mark the location where the Patriots under Colonels Richard Caswell and Arthur Lillington defeated the Loyalists. The reconstruction follows eighteenth-century bridge design and construction techniques, including the use of thick wooden planks and parallel support beams (called "stringers"). The bridge became fully accessible to the public in January 2026.

GRADY MONUMENT / PATRIOT MONUMENT

John Grady, a farmer from Duplin County, was the only Patriot killed during the battle. He was shot as he poked his head above the earthwork to take surer aim at the enemy. No one knows for certain where he is buried; local historians speculate that he may have lingered several days before he died and may have been buried in Wilmington.

On February 27, 1857 (the eighty-first anniversary of the Battle of Moores Creek Bridge), a cornerstone was laid in the presence of the Wilmington Light Infantry, the Wellington Rifle Guards, and a large crowd that had come to participate in the ceremonies.

Within several years, the obelisk was placed on top of the cornerstone and foundation. This monument pays tribute to all Revolutionary War Patriots who sacrificed their lives for independence and the birth of a new nation.

LOYALISTS MONUMENT

Erected by the Moores Creek Monument Association in 1909, this monument honors the Loyalists who fought and died here.

JAMES F. MOORE MONUMENT / BATTLEGROUND ASSOCIATION MONUMENT

James Fulton Moore (1852–1912), the first president of the Moores Creek Battleground Association, helped develop this park as a memorial to the Patriots who fought here. In appreciation of his fourteen years of selfless service, the association erected this eight-foot obelisk soon after his death in July 1912.

ORIGINAL LINE EARTHWORKS

The low earthworks here were hastily erected by the Patriots in preparation for meeting the Loyalist assault.

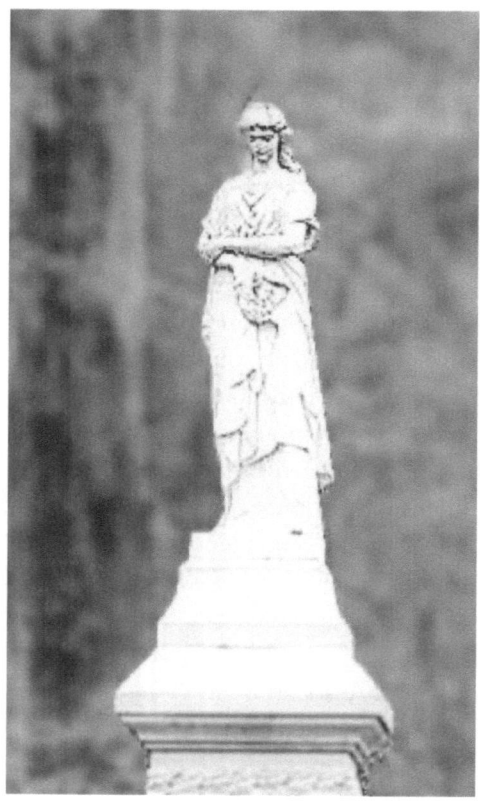

Mary Slocumb Monument / Women's Monument, Moores Creek National Military Park (ALPER)

MARY SLOCUMB MONUMENT / WOMEN'S MONUMENT

A fascinating legend has grown around Mrs. Mary Slocumb, who, having dreamed that her husband lay wounded on the Moores Creek battlefield, rode alone at night for sixty-five miles to tend his injuries. When Mary arrived here, she was relieved to find her husband, Ezekiel, unharmed. She immediately proceeded to give aid to the other soldiers.

In 1907, the Moores Creek Monument Association, with $2,000 appropriated by Congress, erected this statue to Mary Slocumb. It also serves to honor the devoted and self-sacrificing women of the Cape Fear region, and it pays tribute to all women who contributed to Revolutionary War efforts.

SLOCUMB GRAVES

In front of the statue are the graves of Mary (nicknamed "Polly") and Ezekiel Slocumb. Their remains were removed from the cemetery at Mount Olive (around 100 miles to the north) and reinterred here in 1929.

New Bern

REVOLUTIONARY WAR HISTORY

Serving as the Colonial capital of North Carolina, New Bern was the location of the royal governor's official residence. The North Carolina Assembly appropriated £15,000 (around $75,000) for the building of the impressive structure, and construction began in 1767 under the supervision of John Hawks, an English architect. Skilled artisans were brought from England and Pennsylvania, and within three years the luxurious mansion was completed. The first residents were Royal Governor William Tryon, his wife Margaret, and their nine-year-old daughter. In 1771, when Tryon was appointed governor of New York, he and his family moved to that colony.

William Tryon—who served as royal governor of North Carolina from 1764 to 1771—is remembered for suppressing the Regulator Movement, a revolt of backcountry farmers against the corrupt practices of Colonial officials that led to the Battle of Alamance.

Tryon's successor, Josiah Martin, lived in the New Bern Governor's Palace until 1775. After the Patriots of the area received news of the Battles of Lexington and Concord in April 1775, they held Martin prisoner for a short time; soon afterward, he was forced to flee.

On January 16, 1777, Richard Caswell was inaugurated in the palace as governor under the first constitution of the independent state of North Carolina. Three months later, the first state General Assembly was convened, and it continued to meet regularly until 1794, when the state capital was moved to Raleigh.

Although serving for a time as the seat of government of North Carolina, New Bern saw little military involvement in the Revolutionary

War except for a brief occupation in August 1781 by a raiding party from British-held Wilmington. During George Washington's visit to New Bern in April 1791, he was entertained at a banquet and a ball at the Governor's Palace. On the afternoon of Thursday, April 21, an address of welcome was followed by fifteen toasts, each announced by the thunder of cannon. A member of the president's party then read an official reply to the greetings. That evening Washington, clad in black velvet and wearing a powdered wig, attended a ball held in the Council Chamber. The wife of Richard Dobbs Spaight (a signer of the Constitution and later a governor of North Carolina) danced the first minuet with the distinguished guest. Washington's visit was perhaps New Bern's last moment of political glory.

COLONIAL AND REVOLUTIONARY WAR SITES
TRYON PALACE COMPLEX / NORTH CAROLINA HISTORY CENTER

529 South Front Street. Open Monday through Saturday, 10 a.m. to 5 p.m.; Sunday, 12 p.m. to 5 p.m. Closed major holidays. Adults $20, youth (6–14) $10, children (under 5) free. Tours available. Phone: (800) 767-1560. Website: www.tryonpalace.org. Most of the Tryon Palace was destroyed by fire on the night of February 27, 1798. Only the west wing was still standing in 1952 when restoration was begun. It took $4 million and years of dedicated work to restore the buildings and grounds to their original beauty.

The Palace

Re-creation of the interior was aided by the discovery of Governor Tryon's inventory of furnishings.

The **Library**—to the left of the main entrance—contains 400 editions, including volumes of philosophy, history, and military science. Among the interesting items in the room are an eighteenth-century barometer, rare Stuart-period brass candlesticks, a chess table, an Edward Aldridge silver inkstand, and an eglomise painting of Queen Anne.

The **Council Chamber** served a dual purpose: for Royal Council meetings, when the governor and his advisors met to discuss official

Tryon Palace, New Bern (LIBRARY OF CONGRESS, PRINTS AND PHOTOGRAPHS DIVISION)

business, and for state parties and balls. The most distinguished visitor entertained here was George Washington (1791).

Today the room is furnished with a desk and master armchair, a large mahogany table with twelve Gothic Chippendale chairs, and two Irish cut-glass chandeliers. An unusual musical clock (made by Charles Clay of London in 1736) not only records the time, the day of the month, and the phases of the moon but also chimes and plays operatic airs!

The marble mantel is almost an exact duplicate of the one described in Tryon's inventory. Flanking the fireplace are a pair of full-length portraits of King George III and his consort, Queen Charlotte, in their coronation robes. The portraits, painted in England during the 1760s, are attributed to the School of Sir Joshua Reynolds.

The handsome Chippendale table in the **Dining Room** is set for a dessert course—with a Worcester porcelain dessert service and unusual enamel and metal knives and forks. The portrait of Queen Anne (attributed to the School of Sir Godfrey Kneller) honors the patron of

Council Chamber, Tryon Palace (COURTESY OF TRYON PALACE)

Baron Christoph von Graffenried, who founded New Bern in the first decade of the eighteenth century. (He had come from Bern, Switzerland, and named the settlement in honor of his former home.)

In the **Music Room** the women congregated to gossip, sip tea, and hear music. Exhibited here are a spinet (Hitchcock, London, c. 1720), a flute (Camusac, London, c. 1760), and other instruments representative of the period. The dress worn by Eunice Kelley at the gala ball given for George Washington is displayed on a mannequin in one corner of the room. (The dress was in the possession of a local family and was presented to the Tryon Palace Restoration Commission.)

Other distinguished furnishings in the music room are worth noting. The Turkish carpet dates from the sixteenth century; the seven George II chairs—originally made for the Earl of Shaftesbury—are covered in rare Soho tapestry; the elaborately carved mahogany card table with folding top was made by William Vile, a highly respected cabinetmaker to the royal household of King George III; and the painting *Landscape with Huntsmen* is by Claude Lorrain.

Although food was cooked in the east wing, it was brought to the **"Housekeeper's" Room** and placed in warming cupboards before being served. Trays, china, glassware, and dinnerware that once were stored here are now on display. One may also see syllabub glasses (for "syllabub," a dessert of sweetened cream flavored with wine and beaten to a froth) and a silver pap boat (for "pap," bread boiled or softened in milk or water that was fed to infants and invalids). The small chest, or "tea caddy," contains three canisters—one might have held a green tea, the second a black tea, and the third a blend.

The second floor was used for the family quarters. The **Ochre Bedroom** and the **Mauve Bedroom** are furnished with majestic four-poster beds with floral bedspreads, delft washbasins, mirrors, and dressing tables. The **Governor's Bedroom** features an English carved canopy bed (with paw feet and spiral-twist fluting), a Queen Anne bonnet-top highboy, and a portrait of Charles Tryon, father of Royal Governor William Tryon. The **Daughter's Room**—occupied by Tryon's daughter when the family resided here—has dolls, a wooden birdcage, a delicate tea set, and miniature furniture (which originally may have been traveling cabinetmakers' samples).

Visitors may also wish to see the **East Wing**, which houses the kitchen, the secretary's office, and a servants' dining room. Not to be missed are the **Kitchen Garden** (with herbs, vegetables, and fruit trees) and the magnificent **Latham Memorial Garden** (completed in 1959 at a cost of over $1 million).

North Carolina History Center

529 South Front Street. Monday through Saturday, 10 a.m. to 5 p.m.; Sunday, 12 p.m. to 5 pm. One-day pass $20 for adults, $10 for youth (6–14), children (under 5) free. Other passes available at various fees. For information about admission tickets and tours, visit www.tryonpalace.org.

The North Carolina History Center includes the following:

Regional History Museum explores through extraordinary exhibitions five centuries of the history and culture of central and coastal North Carolina.

Pepsi Family Center emphasizes interactive and special-effects displays that are especially appealing to children.

Duffy Gallery offers special touring and rotating exhibitions.

Stanly House

307 George Street. Currently closed to the public, although its gardens are open. This house was designed by John Hawks (architect of Tryon Palace) for his friend John Wright Stanly and was completed in the early 1780s. The center door of the two-story structure is framed with Doric columns supporting a denticulated pediment, and the windows on the first floor have decorative carved moldings. The structure is topped with a hipped roof with a balustrade.

As a young man, Stanly was engaged in the export business in Kingston, Jamaica, and in Philadelphia. In 1772, he was traveling to Charleston, South Carolina, when a violent storm at sea forced him ashore at Beaufort, North Carolina. There John Sitgreaves, a shipboard companion, invited him to settle in New Bern. According to tradition, soon after his arrival in the community, he met Ann Cogdell at a palace ball given by Royal Governor Josiah Martin, fell in love, and married her the next year.

Stanly built a flourishing business; he owned ships engaged in the West Indies trade as well as a local molasses distillery. As the hostilities between the colonies and Britain intensified, he engaged roughly fifteen privateers (privately owned armed ships) to keep the ports of Ocracoke and Cape Lookout open, thereby permitting supplies to move through New Bern. After the war erupted, his ships carried munitions to the Patriots from their French allies and even attacked and captured British ships, confiscating foodstuffs and other items useful to the Patriot cause.

John Wright Stanly also advanced more than $80,000 to General Nathanael Greene to support his military campaigns. The loan was never repaid. After the Revolution, Washington appointed him First Judge of the Maritime Court of North Carolina in gratitude for his wartime services.

Stanly's life was snuffed out prematurely during the yellow fever epidemic of 1789. He died at the age of forty-seven on June 1, 1789; his wife died a month later. Although no one occupied this house for several decades after the demise of the Stanlys, it was the scene of a joyous occasion in 1791. When President George Washington stayed here on April 20–21, the residence was cleaned and new furniture was brought in for his sojourn.

The house, which passed through the hands of many owners, was moved to its present location in 1966 and restored to its original splendor.

Records show that the Stanlys were visited by many distinguished guests. The **Dining Room**—with its Waterford chandelier, fine furniture, Chinese export porcelain, and a portrait of the Washington family (after Edward Savage)—was the center for entertainment. In the evening guests might have played cards in the **Parlor** at the fine gaming table. It stands near a Philadelphia lowboy (by William Savery) and a wing chair covered in its original needlepoint.

The hourglass, telescope, and two globes (London, c. 1770) are appropriate fittings for the **Library** of a ship owner. Near the secretary-bookcase, made by cabinetmaker Thomas Burling of New York, hang engravings of Nathanael Greene and George Washington.

Among the appointments in the **Master Bedroom** are a gentleman's wig stand and two japanned dressing boxes. On the desk is a copy of a letter written by Mrs. Stanly to her husband, scolding him for not writing more frequently and asking him to purchase a pair of shoes for one of the children.

The house, standing on the grounds near Tryon Palace, is an extraordinarily fine restoration.

Stevenson House

609 Pollock Street. Currently closed to the public. A fine example of early nineteenth-century architecture, this dwelling was built by a sea captain whose ships sailed between New Bern and the West Indies. During the War between the States, it was used as a hospital. In 1957, the structure was purchased by the Tryon Palace Commission for restoration.

Today it is furnished with Federal and Empire antiques. Among the outstanding pieces are a pair of Crown Derby urns signed by William Duesbury, a Hepplewhite inlaid mahogany secretary-bookcase, a Sheraton dining table and sideboard from Philadelphia, an Empire gilt chandelier, a mahogany sleigh bed, and rare porcelains.

CHRIST EPISCOPAL CHURCH

320 Pollock Street. Office open Monday through Thursday, 9 a.m. to 3 p.m.; Friday, 9 a.m. to 12 p.m. Phone: (252) 633-2109. The first brick church to stand on this site was completed in 1750. Two years later, King George II presented the parish with a Bible and a silver Communion service, which are still in use today. When Royal Governor Josiah Martin fled from New Bern in May 1775, he tried to confiscate the silver but failed. (During the Civil War, the Communion service was secretly carried to a parish in Fayetteville, where it was hidden.)

The first Christ Episcopal Church was set ablaze by a band of incensed colonists who objected to the royal arms of England being displayed conspicuously above the door. The structure was rebuilt soon after the Revolutionary War. The current Gothic Revival church was built in 1871–1875, incorporating the surviving frame of the previous church (1824), which had burned down.

CLERMONT CEMETERY

1119 Brice's Creek Road. This land was part of the plantation owned by Colonel William Wilson and his wife, Mary Vail. In 1756, their daughter, Elizabeth, married Richard Spaight, a member of the Council of Royal Governor Arthur Dobbs (1757–1766). Their son, Richard Dobbs Spaight (1758–1800), became the first native-born governor of North Carolina (1792–1795). He is buried in this cemetery near his parents.

LADY BLESSINGTON CANNON

New Bern Academy Museum, 508 New Street. Open Saturday and Sunday, 12:30–4:40 p.m. This cannon was captured during the War of Independence from the *Lady Blessington*, a British warship, by one of John Wright Stanly's privateers.

IMPORTANT COLONIAL HOUSES
HAWKS HOUSE

306 Hancock Street. Not open to the public. Built in the mid-1700s, this house was sold in April 1807 to Francis Hawks, son of John Hawks, architect of Tryon Palace.

HOWARD HOUSE

520 New Street. Not open to the public. This handsome Georgian house (built in the early 1770s) was the home of Martin Howard, first master of the local Masonic Lodge.

GASTON HOUSE

421 Craven Street between Broad and Pollock Streets. Not open to the public. This is a reconstruction of the office of Judge William Gaston, a justice of the North Carolina Supreme Court. His father, Alexander, was killed on August 20, 1781, by a Loyalist as he and his family were fleeing to safety. (British soldiers had arrived in New Bern on August 19.) According to tradition, the Gastons escaped through a tunnel running from their house to a small outbuilding, but Alexander Gaston was cut down as he and his family were about to board a boat at the waterfront.

Gaston House, New Bern (LIBRARY OF CONGRESS, PRINTS AND PHOTOGRAPHS DIVISION)

MASONIC MEETING HALL

516 Hancock Street. Not open to the public. This structure served as the meeting place for the local Masonic Lodge. (Chartered in 1772, it is the second-oldest lodge in the state.) The first master was Martin Howard, chief magistrate of the Royal Colony of North Carolina from 1767 to 1773. President Washington met with his Masonic brothers here during his visit to New Bern. A major renovation was undertaken in 1904 and a theater space was added, now home to the River Towne Players.

Edenton

REVOLUTIONARY WAR HISTORY

Ten months after the Boston Tea Party, fifty-one women of the Albemarle region gathered at Edenton to protest the British tea tax and the royal government's harsh policies. The defiant ladies drew up a resolution boycotting East India tea, which prompted one local resident to boast that Edenton possessed "more female artillery" than any other town in America. Among the signers of that resolution at the so-called Edenton Tea Party on October 25, 1774, were Anne Johnston, Abigail Charlton, Penelope Barker, Elizabeth King, Jean Blair, and Sarah Littlejohn.

During the Revolutionary War, a supply depot was located at Edenton. Although British troops never attacked the town, in May 1779 the enemy fleet entered Hampton Roads and took Portsmouth, Virginia. As the vessels sailed toward Suffolk, Virginia, residents of Edenton—fearing that troops would disembark and march southward—loaded their furnishings and belongings onto carts and fled. But the Redcoats never reached the town.

Penelope Barker of the Edenton Tea Party, artist unknown, Barker House (EDENTON HISTORICAL COMMISSION)

In late May 1781, a British galley, the *General Arnold*, slipped into Edenton Harbor at night and made off with the schooner *Small Hopes*, owned by William Littlejohn. The men of Edenton armed several small boats and bravely pursued the galley, which they captured. But they arrived too late to save the American vessel; *Small Hopes* had gone up in smoke.

Several prominent Revolutionary leaders lived in Edenton. Joseph Hewes (1730–1779) served in the North Carolina Assembly (1766–1775), the First Provincial Congress (1775), and the Continental Congress (1774) and was a signer of the Declaration of Independence (1776). He gained the dubious distinction of being the only signer to die in Philadelphia (1779). (Fate seemed to balance things in 1798 when James Wilson, a Pennsylvania signer, died in Edenton while a guest at the James Iredell house.)

VISITOR INFORMATION

Penelope Barker House Welcome Center, 505 South Broad Street; (252) 482-7800. Open daily, 10 a.m. to 5 p.m. Hours may vary by season.

Eden-Chowan Chamber of Commerce, 101 West Water Street; (252) 482-3400

GUIDED TOURS

Historic Edenton Trolley Tour, Monday, Wednesday through Saturday, 10:30 a.m. to 2:30 p.m. Varies by season. Adults $12.50, youth $2.25, children (under 5) free; (252) 482-2637. Tickets can be purchased at the Penelope Barker House Welcome Center.

1758 Cupola House Tour, Friday through Saturday, 11:30 a.m., 12:30 p.m., and 2:30 p.m.; Sunday, 12:30 p.m. and 2:30 p.m. Adults $12.50, youth $5, children (under 5) free.

PUBLIC TRANSPORTATION

Choanoke Public Transportation, (252) 539-2022
Inter-County Public Transportation Authority, (252) 338-4480

The life of Edenton resident Dr. Hugh Williamson (1735–1819)— merchant, writer, and physician—was rich and eventful. While traveling in Europe in 1775, he sent a document to Lord Mansfield, "The Plea of the Colonies," defending the disloyalty and unrest in the colonies. Returning by ship to North Carolina in December 1776, he was captured by the British but managed to escape. Later, he was appointed surgeon general of the North Carolina troops and was ordered to New Bern to vaccinate the soldiers against smallpox. (Immunity to smallpox through inoculation was known in the early eighteenth century—decades before Edward Jenner's experiments in the 1790s.) At the Battle of Camden, Williamson treated many of the wounded. After the war he served as a delegate to Congress (1782–1785, 1787–1788) and was a signer of the Constitution in 1787. In 1789, he attended the Fayetteville Convention and voted for the ratification of the Constitution.

Edenton is rightfully proud of its sons and daughters who served the cause of liberty.

COLONIAL AND REVOLUTIONARY WAR SITES
BARKER HOUSE
505 South Broad Street. Open Monday and Wednesday through Saturday, 10 a.m. to 4 p.m. Hours may vary by season. Free. Phone: (252) 482-7800. This two-story structure was built in 1782 for Thomas Barker, a successful lawyer who took an active role in Colonial politics. Before the Revolutionary War, he served as the London agent for the North Carolina colony. His wife, Penelope, presided over the Edenton Tea Party.

In the early nineteenth century, the building was purchased by Augustus Moore, a prominent judge. Members of his family occupied the house until 1952, when it was purchased and moved to the present site. It is now the headquarters of the Edenton Historical Commission.

CHOWAN COUNTY COURTHOUSE
117 East King Street. Open Tuesday through Saturday, 10 a.m. to 4 p.m. General admission $2.50. Phone: (252) 482-2637. Built in 1767, this structure is the oldest courthouse still in use in North Carolina. The courthouse design is quite sophisticated and is attributed to John Hawks, architect of Tryon Palace in New Bern. The District Court meets here

Chowan County Courthouse, Edenton (LIBRARY OF CONGRESS, PRINTS AND PHOTO-GRAPHS DIVISION)

most Thursdays, and the Superior Court convenes several times a year. For two centuries the same offices have been used by the register of deeds and the clerks of court. The Masons once used the second-floor east room for meetings of Unanimity Lodge.

The courtroom also served as a public meeting hall. When court was in session, the judge presided from the tall chair in the center of the front of the room. On the second floor the large paneled room—which occupies three central bays and the depth of the building—was used as a ballroom for important occasions. President James Monroe danced here during his visit in 1819.

CHOWAN COUNTY JAIL

Off Courthouse Green. Not open to the public. The Chowan County Jail went through renovations in 2018. The site can be seen on the Edenton Museum Trail north of East King Street. One of the oldest jails in the United

States, this white brick building surrounded by high walls was built in 1787. Plans for an Edenton "gaol" were drawn up as early as 1773 by John Hawks (architect of Tryon Palace), but the design was modified by Charles Sheeter, who supervised construction of this structure. Today it is used for offices.

COURTHOUSE GREEN
Revolutionary War Cannon
The cannon facing the waterfront were salvaged from a shipment of armaments carried on a French vessel that sank in Albemarle Sound in 1778. They had been purchased by Benjamin Franklin, Arthur Lee, and Silas Deane, who were the American commissioners to France.

Teapot Memorial
This small bronze teapot on a five-foot pole marks the site of the home of Mrs. Elizabeth King, where fifty-one Edenton women met in 1774 to protest the high taxes on tea.

CUPOLA HOUSE
408 South Broad Street. Open Friday and Saturday, 11:30 a.m. to 3:30 p.m.; Sunday, 12:30 p.m. to 3 p.m. Adults $12.50, children (under 5) free, youth (6–17) $5. Phone: (252) 482-2637. House contents may vary. Gardens are open daily. Named for the small octagonal structure surmounting the roof, the Cupola House was built for a sea captain, Richard Sanderson, around 1725. The building is characterized by prominent gables and a second-floor overhang. The interior woodwork was probably added in the late 1750s by Francis Corbin, an agent for Lord Granville, one of the Lords Proprietor. Corbin had the finial on the front of the house added; it bears the initials "F.C." and the date 1758. His heirs sold the house in 1777 to Dr. Samuel Dickinson, who lived here with his eleven children. His descendants resided here for 141 years. Since the original woodwork was purchased and removed by the Brooklyn Museum, the woodwork on the first floor is a reproduction. Especially fine are the moldings around the windows, the rosettes and designs above the built-in cupboards, the carving of the doors, and the elaborate mantels.

The fireplace in the **Main Room** has a fireback with an oak tree depicted on it. It is dated 1660, with the initials "C.R." for "Charles Rex." According to legend, King Charles II (1630–1685) saved his life during a battle by hiding in the branches of an oak tree. The fireback has a dual purpose: to protect the back of the fireplace and to throw off heat.

The room is furnished with eighteenth-century pieces. The china on the Queen Anne tea table once belonged to the Dickinson family. The portrait of Penelope Barker, displayed here for decades, was moved to the Barker House.

In the **Hall** hangs a portrait of Thomas Hodgson (by Wollaston), Penelope Barker's nephew and stepson. (Thomas was the son of Penelope's sister. After her sister's death, the widowed Penelope married the father of Thomas, thereby becoming his stepmother and aunt at the same time.) The calendar clock is the only piece of furniture that has remained

Cupola House, Edenton (LIBRARY OF CONGRESS, PRINTS AND PHOTOGRAPHS DIVISION)

in this house since the eighteenth century. It was purchased in England for Dr. Dickinson by Charles Pettygrove.

The comfortable **Sitting Room** has a wing chair (1740) covered in crewel and a fine Chippendale secretary. The little "toddy" table, made in Edenton in the early 1700s, is one of the few North Carolina pieces in this dwelling. Several of the pictures are painted on the reverse side of the glass, a popular technique of the eighteenth century.

Articles discovered in the house during the restoration are on display in Dr. Dickinson's **Study**: four antique maps, a three-footed child's bench, a trunk, a footwarmer, and a newspaper—dated 1797. One item of unusual interest is the three-sided crib, which could be either pulled up to the mother's bed at night or placed against a wall during the day to ensure the infant's safety.

The upstairs **Dressing Room** contains a dress worn by the wife of James Iredell (associate justice of the Supreme Court, appointed by George Washington). The pencil-post bed in the **Master Bedroom** has an unusual bedspread of pieced appliqué on a white background. On the Queen Anne commode chair near the elm highboy, a doll with china feet is perched. This doll was typical of those sent by English merchants to model the latest London fashions, which could be purchased and shipped to the colonies.

Two delightful items in the upstairs rooms are a decorated patch box used for keeping the fake beauty marks women wore and a 1794 valentine with a poem ending, "And if these fair lines you do refuse / Pray burn the paper and me excuse."

From the **Servants' Quarters** on the third floor—where objects such as a pewter bedpan, an old sewing machine, and a wine press are stored—one can climb a circular barrel staircase into the cupola to be rewarded with a panoramic view of Edenton.

IREDELL HOUSE

107 East Church Street. Can be seen on the Edenton Museum Trail and through the Penelope Barker Welcome Center Tour. When seventeen-year-old James Iredell came to America from England in 1751, he was ready to assume his duties as deputy collector for the port of Roanoke. He studied law and eleven years later became attorney general of North Carolina. Following the Revolutionary War, he was appointed associate justice of the US Supreme Court by George Washington.

In 1778, five years after his marriage to Hannah Johnston (sister of future governor Samuel Johnston), Iredell purchased this property from local silversmith Joseph Whedbee. The structure was significantly enlarged in 1799 by a two-story addition and porches.

The house passed through the hands of several owners (in the 1850s, it was used as a rectory for St. Paul's) until the Edenton Chapter of the Daughters of the American Revolution purchased it in 1949.

This structure underwent a significant restoration in 2024, and it features superb period furnishings.

ST. PAUL'S EPISCOPAL CHURCH

101 West Gale Street. Services available Sunday, 8 a.m. and 11 a.m. Service times are subject to change. Phone: (252) 482-3522. Organized under the Vestry Act of 1701, St. Paul's parish holds one of the oldest charters in North Carolina. The church building, which was completed in 1760, fell into disrepair and was restored between 1806 and 1809. Four decades later, the present chancel woodwork was added.

While the church was being refurbished in 1949, fire destroyed the roof and steeple, but since the furnishings had already been removed, they were not damaged. Among the cherished possessions of St. Paul's Church are a book of vestry minutes (1701), a silver chalice and paten (1725), an alms basin (c. 1812), and a pair of silver-plated vases (1852).

Several Revolutionary War leaders were members of this parish: Joseph Hewes (a signer of the Declaration of Independence), James Iredell (a lawyer who became associate justice of the first US Supreme Court), and Samuel Johnston (clerk of the Superior Court, later a governor of North Carolina and senator from the state).

A large group of colonists convened here in 1774 to elect delegates to the Provincial Congress. On June 19, 1776—two weeks before the adoption of the Declaration of Independence—parishioners signed "The Test," a document protesting unfair English taxation policies and supporting the actions of the Continental Congress. In the churchyard are buried three Colonial governors, all members of St. Paul's: Thomas Pollock, Henderson Walker, and Charles Eden, for whom Edenton was named. (Until 1725, the year of Eden's death, the village had been called Queen Anne's Town.)

IMPORTANT COLONIAL HOUSES

CHARLTON HOUSE

West Eden Street near South Granville Street. Not open to the public. Jasper Charlton, owner of this home, was active in Revolutionary politics. His wife, Abigail, is said to have been the first signer of the "Tea Party" Resolutions.

BENNETT-DIXON HOUSE

West Queen Street between South Broad and South Granville Streets. Not open to the public. William Bennett, a member of the North Carolina Committee of Safety, bought this dwelling in the early 1770s. His wife, Lydia, was a signer of the "Tea Party" Resolutions.

MILLEN HOUSE

East Water Street between South Oakun and Court Streets. Not open to the public. Quentin Millen, a successful merchant, built a house on this site in the early 1770s. A fiery Loyalist, he was forced to leave the country during the Revolution, although his family remained in Edenton.

PAXTON-MCCULLOCH HOUSE

West King Street between South Broad and South Granville Streets. Not open to the public. This house was owned by Henry Eustace McCulloch, a cousin of James Iredell. Loyal to England, McCulloch returned home when hostilities in the colonies began to intensify. His property was confiscated during the War of Independence.

PEMBROKE HALL

West King Street between South Broad and South Granville Streets. Not open to the public. In the mid-eighteenth century, this property was bought by

Thomas Childs, one of Lord Granville's agents. During the Revolution the house was occupied by Mrs. Mary Littledale, one of the organizers of the Edenton Tea Party and a signer of the Resolutions. The current structure dates from the 1850s.

WESSINGTON-EVERARD HOUSE
120 West King Street. Not open to the public. The house originally on this site was the residence of Sir Richard Everard, royal governor of North Carolina (1725–1731). During the Revolutionary War it was occupied by George Russell, a sea captain, who is remembered for his generous gift of the master's chair to the local Masonic Lodge.

VIRGINIA

Williamsburg

REVOLUTIONARY WAR HISTORY

After the Indian Massacre of 1622 at Jamestown (Virginia's capital), a palisade was built across the narrow peninsula between the James and York Rivers. Many colonists then moved to the safety of the higher ground and established a settlement along the palisade called Middle Plantation.

Here in 1676 Nathaniel Bacon (1647–1676) and discontented frontiersmen met to plan a revolt against Royal Governor William Berkeley. High taxes, patronage of a favored clique, and vacillation in establishing adequate frontier defenses led to the uprising. Berkeley was forced to flee but soon regained power after Bacon contracted malaria and died, leaving the insurrectionists without a strong leader. The chief rebels were captured, declared traitors, and hanged.

In 1693, Middle Plantation was chosen as the site of the College of William and Mary (the second-oldest college in the country, preceded only by Harvard). Five years later, after the Jamestown State House was destroyed by fire, the legislators voted to move the seat of government to Middle Plantation, which they renamed Williamsburg in honor of King William III. The new capital—gradually developing into a town of about 200 houses and 1,500 residents—became the political, social, and cultural center of Virginia.

Delegates elected to the House of Burgesses met in Williamsburg twice a year, in April and October. During these "Publick Times" the population of the town swelled to between 6,000 and 8,000.

The colony's first printing press was brought here in 1736 by William Parks, who published Virginia's first newspaper. Before the Revolution,

Patrick Henry made fiery speeches against the British in the Capitol; Thomas Jefferson, Peyton Randolph, and their compatriots formed a Committee of Correspondence; and the House of Burgesses adopted the Virginia Resolution for American Independence, which called on the Continental Congress to sever all ties with England.

But the glory that was Williamsburg came to an end in 1780 when the seat of government was transferred to Richmond. Many of Williamsburg's handsome buildings then fell into disrepair; others burned to the ground.

In 1926, John D. Rockefeller Jr. and Dr. W. A. R. Goodwin, rector of Bruton Parish Church, initiated plans for the restoration of Colonial Williamsburg. After years of painstaking historical and archaeological research, the rebuilding and renovations began. Today, the Historic Area covers around 170 acres, extending one mile in length. Eighty-five eighteenth-century houses, taverns, shops, and public buildings have been restored, and fifty important structures have been rebuilt on their original sites.

VISITOR INFORMATION

Colonial Williamsburg Regional Visitor Center, 101 Visitor Center Drive; (888) 965-7254

Visit Williamsburg, 421 North Boundary Street; (757) 229-6511

Colonial Williamsburg tickets can be purchased at the visitor center or at www.colonialwilliamsburg.org. Single-day tickets for adults $37.50, youth (6–12) $10, children (under 5) free. Multiday passes for adults $55, youth (6–12) $28. Other unique ticket options are available online for Virginia residents.

GUIDED TOURS

Tour of Colonial Williamsburg
Colonial Williamsburg Ghost Stories and Walking Tour
Colonial Tour in Williamsburg
Arrangements for all the above tours can be made through Viator (855-275-5071) or at the reception desk in the visitor center.

WALKING TOURS

Most of Williamsburg's major points of interest can be seen in two
  walking tours. (During summer, entrance lines may be long,
  so visitors should p an accordingly. A minimum of two days is
  suggested.)

Tour A

*Area bounded by Lafayette Street on the north, Francis Street on the
south, Queen Street on the east, and Nassau Street on the west.*

Start at north end of the Palace Green.

Governor's Palace

Brush-Everard House

Peyton-Randolph House

Courthouse

Magazine

James Geddy House

Bruton Parish Church

George Wythe House

(Craft shops in the area include those of the bootmaker, weaver,
cooper, and basket maker.)

End on the west side of the Palace Green.

Tour B

*Area bounded by Nicholson Street on the north, Francis Street on the
south, Waller Street on the east, and Botetourt Street on the west.*

Start on Duke of Gloucester Street, just east of Botetourt Street

Wetherburn's Tavern

Raleigh Tavern

Capitol

Public Gaol

(Craft shops in the area include those of the jeweler, wigmaker, and
gunsmith; also the bakery and the apothecary.)

End on Nicholson Street, just north of the Capitol.

WILLIAMSBURG SITES
BRUSH-EVERARD HOUSE

214 Palace Green Street. Built in 1717, this small structure served as the residence and workshop of John Brush, an armorer and gunsmith who also served as the first keeper of the Williamsburg Magazine. At that time the dwelling consisted of one room on each side of a central hall and a loft.

Around mid-century the property was acquired by Thomas Everard, who held several important civic positions, including clerk of the General Court and mayor of Williamsburg. He enlarged the house by adding two wings to the rear, creating the U-shaped structure. The interior was enhanced by an elaborate staircase and fine woodwork.

Today the rooms are furnished with antiques of the period. Of special interest is the **Child's Room** (on the second floor) with its miniature furniture and accessories. The **Library** is stocked with roughly 300 books, reproducing as nearly as possible Everard's fine collection (which was purchased after his death by Thomas Jefferson).

Bruton Parish Church, Colonial Williamsburg (LIBRARY OF CONGRESS, PRINTS AND PHOTOGRAPHS DIVISION)

BRUTON PARISH CHURCH

201 Duke of Gloucester Street. Open Monday through Friday, 8 a.m. to 4 p.m. Tours are available on www.brutonparish.org. Phone: (757) 229-2891. Organized in 1674, Bruton Parish was named for an English parish in Somerset, the native home of several prominent residents of the Virginia colony. The present brick church, completed in 1715, was designed by Royal Governor Alexander Spotswood. The altar was placed at the east end, and a special area was set aside for the use of the governor and his council. Because of the rapidly growing congregation, the church was enlarged in 1744. The first organ was installed in 1755, and the bell (presented to the parish by local merchant James Tarpley) was mounted in the steeple in 1761.

After reports arrived in Williamsburg in 1774 that Parliament had closed the Port of Boston, the burgesses proclaimed June 1 a day of fasting and prayer with services at Bruton Parish. Years later, the church bell rang out the news of the adoption of the Declaration of Independence (1776) and the signing of the Treaty of Paris formally ending the Revolutionary War (1783).

Among the important political leaders who worshipped here were George Washington, Thomas Jefferson, George Mason, Patrick Henry, James Madison, and James Monroe.

CAPITOL

64 East Duke of Glouster Street. Open daily, 9 a.m. to 5 p.m. Construction of the Capitol began in 1701 under the supervision of master builder Henry Cary. The building was laid out in the shape of an H—two wings with a connecting section. One wing housed the Hall of Burgesses and committee rooms; the other contained the General Courtroom and Council Chamber. When fire destroyed the structure in 1747, Royal Governor William Gooch ordered it rebuilt. The second Capitol, which was completed in 1753, fell into disrepair after the government moved to Richmond in 1780. It burned to the ground in the early nineteenth century.

The first Capitol has been reconstructed on the site, and it is one of America's most cherished historical shrines.

In this building representatives convened from the entire Virginia colony (which at one time stretched almost to the Ohio River). Burgesses, who were elected for one-year terms, traveled to Williamsburg twice a year—in April and October, the "Publick Times"—when the House of Burgesses sat to consider legislation. A bill was read in the House of Burgesses and then assigned to one of six standing committees. After the language was refined, amendments added, and revisions completed, the bill was read twice more in the House to be adopted or dismissed. Once passed, major bills were sent to England for the king's signature.

The day-to-day affairs of government were superseded by a crisis of immense proportions when the British Parliament passed the Stamp Act in 1765. Young Patrick Henry delivered an impassioned oration here protesting the policies of the mother country. Several conservative burgesses interrupted with cries of "Treason," to which Henry retorted, "If this be Treason, make the most of it."

In 1776, when relations between England and the colonies had passed the point of compromise, the burgesses selected Edmund Pendleton to draft the document that became known as the "Virginia Resolution for American Independence." It was introduced to the Continental Congress in Philadelphia by the Virginia delegation. When they returned home, the burgesses asked George Mason to form a committee

Patrick Henry at the Virginia House of Burgesses,
engraving by Alfred Jones after P. F. Rothermel
(LIBRARY OF CONGRESS, PRINTS AND PHOTOGRAPHS
DIVISION)

to draft a constitution for Virginia, thus signifying the official ending of the role of England in their internal affairs. In June 1776, Patrick Henry was elected to serve as the first American governor of the newly established commonwealth.

Sessions of the General Court (the highest in the territory) were held concurrently with the sitting of the House of Burgesses. The royal governor and twelve counselors (who were appointed for life by the Crown) presided in the paneled courtroom, where they heard criminal cases involving loss of life or limb and civil cases amounting to more than £10. After a trial, the jurors (who had been brought to Williamsburg at public expense) retired to a third-floor chamber, without benefit of food or drink, to consider their verdicts. Not until the last day of court were all sentences passed.

COURTHOUSE

101 West Duke of Gloucester Street. Open daily, 9 a.m. to 5 p.m. Constructed in 1770 to replace an earlier courthouse (at Francis and England Streets), this building housed the county and the municipal courts. The structure is typical of Colonial Virginia courthouses: It is built on a T-shaped design and has arched windows and a cupola. In 1911, columns were added to the overhanging pediment, but they were removed in 1932 when the building was restored to its original eighteenth-century appearance.

The square on which the courthouse stands was the site of town fairs (in April and December) and served as a farmers' market. Here, too, local militiamen mustered. In July 1776, the Declaration of Independence was read in the square, and the joyous event was celebrated with fireworks and the salute of guns.

The interior of the building is now being renovated; it will be furnished in the style of a local eighteenth-century courthouse.

JAMES GEDDY HOUSE

117 West Duke of Gloucester Street. Open Wednesday through Sunday, 9 a.m. to 5 p.m. Gunsmith James Geddy, a Scottish immigrant, settled in a small house on this site in the late 1730s. In 1750, six years after his death, Geddy's widow built the present two-story house and the one-and-a-half-story extension. A son, James, purchased the property in 1760 and established his residence and shop here. Becoming one of Williamsburg's most successful metalworkers, James Geddy II not only crafted utensils of pewter and brass but also fashioned fine jewelry of silver and gold. A respected member of the community, he was elected to the city's Common Council.

The house is a rare example of eighteenth-century Williamsburg architecture because of its L-shaped plan, low-pitched roof without dormers, and front porch crowned with a balcony. The furniture—mostly Colonial American—reflects the economic and social status of a prosperous eighteenth-century craftsman.

GOVERNOR'S PALACE

Facing the Palace Green. Open daily 10 a.m.–5 p.m. In 1706, the House of Burgesses granted £3,000 for construction of an official governor's mansion. Henry Cary, architect and master builder, was appointed overseer of the project. Because of innumerable crises—lack of sufficient funds, incompetence of the workmen, and delivery of damaged materials—the Governor's Palace was not completed until 1720.

The most elegant building in Williamsburg, the palace was the home of seven royal governors: Alexander Spotswood, 1720–1722; Hugh Drysdale, 1722–1726; William Gooch, 1727–1749; Robert Dinwiddie, 1751–1758; Francis Fauquier, 1758–1768; Norborne Berkeley, Baron de Botetourt, 1768–1770; John Murray, Earl of Dunmore, 1771–1775.

The last royal governor of Virginia, who in his zealous execution of British edicts had incurred the wrath of the colonists, found it expedient to secretly flee the palace one night in June 1775 and take refuge on a British man-of-war anchored in Chesapeake Bay.

The first two governors of the independent commonwealth of Virginia also occupied this mansion: Patrick Henry, 1776–1779, and Thomas Jefferson, 1779–1780. In 1780, the capital was moved from Williamsburg to Richmond because of the presence of the British fleet off the Virginia coast. The Governor's Palace was then converted into a

Governor's Palace, Colonial Wi liamsburg (LIBRARY OF CONGRESS, PRINTS AND PHOTOGRAPHY DIVISION)

hospital for wounded Patriot soldiers; it was destroyed in 1781 through the carelessness of patients.

The east wing was originally used to house the offices of the governor, the lieutenant gove:nor, and a staff of secretaries (who ma:/ have lived in the quarters on the second floor).

The main building, with its cupola rising above the balustraded roof, is furnished with magnificent antiques. The **Little Dining Room**, used by the governor and his family, contains a mahogany Chippendale table and Queen Anne chairs with the original needlework seats. The tea set on the mantel is Whieldon agateware. Dominating the **Great Bedchamber** is an impressive four-poster oak bed (six feet long by five feet wide) that was made in England in the seventeenth century. The cheston-chest, made by a Boston cabinetmaker, is a rare example of this type. In the **Governor's Study** is found the only original piece of furniture from the palace—the tall-case clock that once was the property of Royal Governor Dunmore.

Through the **Ballroom** doorway—now flanked by Allan Ramsey's coronation portraits of George III and Queen Charlotte—passed Virginia's most distinguished residents to enjoy an evening of music and dancing. The most elaborate celebration was held on the king's birthday, when fireworks blazed through the night sky above the palace and guests glided across the dance floor beneath the ballroom chandeliers.

The **Supper Room**, used for receptions or for refreshments during balls, shows a strong Chinese influence: pagoda-like pediments above the doorway, hand-painted wallpaper with Oriental nature motifs, and Chinese-style Chippendale furniture.

In the formal gardens behind the palace, a plot of ground is marked by a simple plaque to commemorate the burial place of 156 Revolutionary War soldiers, some of whom were probably veterans of the Yorktown campaign. A holly maze, similar to the one at Hampton Court, England, provides a pleasurable game for visitors who wish to try to make their way through its labyrinthine pathways.

MAGAZINE

102 East Duke of Gloucester Street. Occasional ongoing restoration. Check hours. The octagonal brick magazine was built in 1715 on the orders of Royal Governor Alexander Spotswood as a central military warehouse for arms and ammunition used in defense against Indian attacks, slave uprisings, and pirate raids.

Six decades later, on the eve of the Revolutionary War, Lord Dunmore, royal governor of Virginia, directed that munitions be removed from the magazine and transferred to a British ship. Irate colonists marched on Williamsburg, demanding either return of the supplies or full payment. Restitution was made, and the mob dispersed.

The magazine, which is the original structure, now houses an outstanding collection of eighteenth-century pistols and muskets.

PEYTON RANDOLPH HOUSE

101 East Nicholson Street. Open Tuesday and Thursday through Sunday, 9 a.m. to 5 p.m. This was the residence of one of Williamsburg's most distinguished citizens, Peyton Randolph (1721–1775), who served as a

Reenactment at the Magazine, Colonial Williamsburg (CAROL M. HIGHSMITH ARCHIVE, LIBRARY OF CONGRESS)

Speaker of the House of Burgesses for a decade preceding the Revolutionary War, was chosen chairman of the Virginia Committee of Correspondence, and was elected president of the First Continental Congress.

In 1715, Randolph's father built the western section—a two-story house with a central chimney—and in 1724, he acquired the one-and-a-half-story dwelling standing on the neighboring lot. Several years later, these two structures were linked by a two-story middle section.

Before the outbreak of the Revolution, Patriots frequently held meetings at this house. On one occasion Randolph read aloud Thomas Jefferson's document known as "A Summary View of the Rights of British America."

While attending the Second Continental Congress, Peyton Randolph died, and his body was sent back from Philadelphia to be buried at the College of William and Mary in Williamsburg. His home continued to be occupied by his widow, the former Elizabeth Harrison

Peyton Randolph, by Goodman and Piggott, after C. W. Peale (LIBRARY OF CONGRESS, PRINTS AND PHOTOGRAPHS DIVISION)

(sister of Benjamin Harrison, a signer of the Declaration of Independence). In October 1824, Lafayette was a guest here while visiting the town.

The interior contains some of the finest paneled rooms in Williamsburg. Among the noteworthy furnishings are an octagonal George II walnut dining table, a silver punch bowl by Richard Gurney and Thomas Cook (London, c. 1740), an imposing English carved mahogany bookcase (c. 1765), an Ushak carpet with an arabesque design (late 1600s), a portrait by eighteenth-century artist Matthew Pratt, and an unusual single-legged corner table with a shell and C-scroll carved on the knee.

PUBLIC GAOL

461 East Nicholson Street. Open daily, 9 a.m. to 5 p.m. The public gaol (jail), completed in 1704, was designed by Henry Cary, the master builder who supervised the construction of the Capitol and the Governor's Palace. In 1722, quarters for the keeper—a lifetime political appointee—were added to this small brick structure. Three types of prisoners were incarcerated here: debtors, persons accused of minor offenses, and those convicted of major crimes.

Debtors, held here for twenty days, were expected to pay their debts after release. For other offenses, such as disturbing the peace and wife-beating, men served sentences of several weeks with some time spent in the pillories and stocks. Persons convicted of major crimes, such as treason, arson, and murder, were shackled in leg irons and held in separate cells until they were hanged.

During the War of Independence, this jail was crowded with spies, Loyalists, and British soldiers.

RALEIGH TAVERN

413 East Duke of Gloucester Street. Open daily, 9 a.m. to 4 p.m. This tavern was named for Sir Walter Raleigh (1552–1618), the English courtier, navigator, and poet of the court of Elizabeth I.

The **Ballroom** and **Apollo Room** were the settings for significant historical events. In 1769, Royal Governor Botetourt, outraged at the colonists' protest against the British Revenue Act, dissolved the Virginia legislature, but the resolute burgesses reconvened at the Raleigh Tavern, where they planned a boycott of British goods. Four years later, several Patriots, including Thomas Jefferson and Patrick Henry, met here to organize the Virginia Committee of Correspondence. When the British closed the Port of Boston in 1774, Virginia leaders congregated at the Raleigh Tavern to determine a course of action.

Many joyous occasions were celebrated here. Peyton Randolph, the first president of the Continental Congress, was honored at a banquet after returning from Philadelphia in 1774. When, in 1783, the Treaty of Paris was signed ending the Revolutionary War, local citizens paraded through the streets and then attended an elaborate reception at the Raleigh. During his visit to Williamsburg in 1824, Lafayette was feted in the Apollo Room by the gentlemen of the community.

This building, which was erected around 1740, was destroyed by fire in 1859. It was not reconstructed until 1930. A significant renovation occurred in 2017. The tavern boasts an outstanding collection of eighteenth-century furniture of English and American origin.

WETHERBURN'S TAVERN

406 East Duke of Gloucester Street. Occasional ongoing restoration. Check hours. Henry Wetherburn, one of the most successful innkeepers in eighteenth-century Williamsburg, gained his wealth and influence through two marriages. In 1738, he married the widow of a tavern proprietor and landowner. A week after her death in 1751, he married the widow of another prosperous innkeeper, thereby acquiring a controlling interest in a second business.

Wetherburn's Tavern has been in continuous use for more than 200 years. The eastern section, the earliest part of the structure, was built around 1740; the western extension was added ten years later. The detailed inventory made at the time of Wetherburn's death in 1760 served as a guide in furnishing the restored tavern.

During "Publick Times," when the burgesses converged on Williamsburg, Wetherburn's Tavern was bustling with activity.

In the **Great Room**—with its fine Chippendale-style tables and chairs set around a marble fireplace—gentlemen would dine, drink, and discuss politics. On the center table sits a delft punch bowl decorated with scenes of the Seven Years' War. When William Randolph III and Peter Jefferson (father of Thomas) were involved in a land transaction in the 1740s, they sealed their agreement over glasses served from this bowl.

The **Middle Room**, or Club Room, was reserved for gambling. The gaming tables here (made in England) have three surfaces—the regular tabletop, one for backgammon, and another for cards. The corner cabinet displays valuable pieces of ceramic and crystal.

The small room on the first floor is known as **Mr. Page's Room** because Colonel John Page rented this chamber by the year to be sure of accommodations whenever he visited Williamsburg on business.

Fourteen beds were placed in the **Bedrooms** on the second floor. It was often necessary for two or three persons to share a bed; sometimes beds were even used in shifts!

In 1751, the tavern was the setting for a banquet honoring newly appointed Governor Dinwiddie. George Washington, who served in the House of Burgesses from 1759 to 1774, frequently dined here.

GEORGE WYTHE HOUSE
112 Palace Green Street. Open Monday, Wednesday, Friday through Saturday, 9 a.m. to 5 p.m. In 1754, George Wythe (1726–1806) settled in Williamsburg and soon married Elizabeth Taliaferro, whose father, Colonel Richard Taliaferro, designed this dignified Georgian mansion for the young couple.

Wythe became one of the most influential men in the colony. A burgess during the years preceding the Revolution, he fought for the rights and independence of the colonies. He later served as mayor of Williamsburg and Chancery Court judge. It was appropriate that he should be the first delegate from Virginia to sign the Declaration of Independence and that he should be a member of the Federal Convention of 1787, which framed the United States Constitution. From 1779 to 1790, he was professor of law at the College of William and Mary, where he taught John Marshall (who became chief justice of the United States Supreme Court) and Henry Clay (who became secretary of state). The young Thomas Jefferson spent several winters in Williamsburg studying law with Wythe, whom he called "my faithful and beloved mentor."

Wythe's house was used by George Washington as his headquarters prior to the Battle of Yorktown, and the Comte de Rochambeau was a guest here after the British surrender.

In 1806, at the age of eighty, Wythe died as a result of a bizarre incident. He was poisoned by his grand-nephew George Sweeney,

George Wythe House, Interior Room, Colonial Williamsburg (LIBRARY OF CONGRESS, PRINTS AND PHOTOGRAPHS DIVISION)

who, finding himself hopelessly in debt, expected to inherit a substantial fortune as his uncle's principal beneficiary. But Wythe survived several days—long enough to change his will. Because the only witness to the crime was a Black woman whose testimony was deemed inadmissible by the court, Sweeney was never convicted.

RECOMMENDED SIDE TRIP
CARTER'S GROVE PLANTATION

Carter's Grove Plantation is located at 8797 Pocahontas Trail, off US 60. A private residence, closed to the public.

The magnificent Georgian mansion of this estate was built in the 1750s by Carter Burwell, a member of the House of Burgesses. He was the grandson of Robert "King" Carter, one of Virginia's wealthiest and most powerful men.

Both George Washington and Thomas Jefferson visited here frequently. According to legend, both men proposed to their sweethearts and were rebuffed in the room now known as the "Refusal Room." Another legend attached to the house tells that ruthless British officer Colonel Banastre Tarleton charged his horse up the stairway, hacking the balustrade with his saber.

In 1927–1928, the roof of the mansion was raised to provide additional space, dormers were introduced, and units connecting the main structure with its dependencies were built.

In 2007, a tech entrepreneur purchased this property as a private residence and a horse breeding farm. Because of financial issues, he was forced to sell it to Samuel M. Mencoff in 2014.

Yorktown

REVOLUTIONARY WAR HISTORY

By midsummer 1781, American morale had reached a low point. Despite military advances, the colonists had begun to weary of the war, and securing financial aid and recruiting fighting men were becoming increasingly difficult. Although George Washington had approximately 3,500 Continentals at his command, he knew that an offensive action would have to be taken if the will to win was to be maintained.

In early August, Washington received a communication that the Comte de Grasse, commanding the French fleet, was preparing to sail from the West Indies toward Virginia. Washington determined that the time was appropriate for decisive action.

The British troops under Charles Cornwallis were at that time garrisoned in Yorktown. Washington sent orders south to Lafayette to prevent Cornwallis from withdrawing into North Carolina. Then, on August 20, after having joined with the French forces under General de Rochambeau near New York City, Washington began to march the Allied troops toward Virginia, where they planned to rendezvous with the French fleet. As they moved southward, their ranks were swelled by local militiamen who were persuaded to join in this campaign.

When the British became cognizant of the Allied strategy, a combined fleet under Admirals Hood and Graves was dispatched from New York with orders to keep de Grasse from entering Chesapeake Bay. On September 5, 1781, the two fleets met outside Hampton Roads, Virginia. The superior strength of the French fleet won the engagement, and Admiral de Grasse was able to not only sail up the bay but also disembark 3,000 troops to join Lafayette. On September 14, the combined

American and French armies had arrived at Williamsburg, twelve miles from Yorktown.

When, on September 28, the Allied armies approached Yorktown, their strength totaled 16,650 men. Of these 8,850 were Americans, commanded by Washington, and 7,800 were French, under Rochambeau. Their foe, Cornwallis, was in command of roughly 6,000 soldiers.

To defend Yorktown, the British general ordered a series of redoubts, earthworks, and batteries constructed around the town. Redoubts 9 and 10, on the eastern end of the British line, and the Fusiliers' Redoubt, on the extreme northwest, were the most heavily manned. The Allied army took positions extending in a six-mile curve from the York River above the town to Wormley Creek in the south.

On the morning of September 30, the Allies were surprised to discover that Cornwallis had evacuated all his outer defense posts except Redoubts 9 and 10 and the Fusiliers' Redoubt. The action was mistakenly construed as a retreat, but Cornwallis had received a dispatch from General Henry Clinton stating that a large fleet and 5,000 men would soon be sailing to relieve the beleaguered army. (Clinton was unable to fulfill his promise immediately, though, and the fleet set sail the same day the British surrendered.)

Battle of Virginia Capes (Chesapeake Bay) by V. Zveg (HAMPTON ROADS NAVAL MUSEUM)

The Americans and French, taking advantage of the British withdrawal, seized the abandoned outposts and began constructing additional redoubts, batteries, and trenches.

By the end of the first week in October, a line of fortifications nearly 2,000 yards long had been erected parallel to the British main defense line. French soldiers took up positions on the left half of the siege line, and the Americans took positions on the right.

Throughout October 9 and 10, Allied guns fired on the town, badly damaging British artillery and setting three enemy ships anchored in the York River ablaze. The Allies then moved their positions forward toward the British camp and constructed a second siege line. Now that they were within reach of Redoubts 9 and 10, the American and French troops prepared to attack.

On the night of October 14, the French forces (under Colonel Guillaume de Deux Ponts) stormed Redoubt 9. In less than thirty minutes they crashed through the abatis, dashed on the redoubt, and mounted the parapet. The simultaneous attack launched by the Americans against Redoubt 10 (under Lieutenant Colonel Alexander Hamilton) lasted only ten minutes. Their bayonet charge pushed across the ditch and into the fortification, creating havoc among the enemy.

On the morning of October 16, Cornwallis sent forth a detachment of 350 men in retaliation for the attack. Lieutenant Colonel Abercrombie led an assault on the batteries of the American second line, spiked four guns, and routed the soldiers. But the British initiative was soon repulsed.

Realizing the hopelessness of his situation, Cornwallis decided that the only way to avoid the annihilation of his army would be to cross the York River to Gloucester Point and retreat northward toward Clinton's army. The plan was for the boats to transport the soldiers to the opposite shore and then return to Yorktown. The action was to continue until the entire force had been evacuated. Under the cover of darkness, the first British regiments embarked, but a sudden storm scattered the boats, driving many of them down the river and causing the maneuver to be discontinued.

General Charles Cornwallis by Thomas Gainsborough (NATURAL PORTRAIT GALLERY, LONDON)

The Allies again began to bombard the town on the morning of October 17. A red-coated drummer boy soon appeared on the parapet and beat a "parley." The Americans finally understood the message and ceased fire. A British officer, under protection of a white flag, was brought blindfolded to Washington's camp, where he asked for a short armistice and the appointment of commissioners to discuss terms of surrender.

The next day the commissioners met at the Moore House and drew up the Articles of Capitulation.

At 2 p.m. on October 19, 1781, the British marched out from Yorktown. In a large field selected for the occasion, the defeated army marched between two lines of Allied troops. Cornwallis, claiming illness, sent Brigadier General Charles O'Hara to tender his sword in surrender. Washington refused to accept the sword from a subordinate officer and directed O'Hara to present it instead to his second-in-command, Major General Benjamin Lincoln.

A total of 7,247 soldiers and 840 seamen surrendered; 244 pieces of artillery and thousands of small arms were captured. Casualties from the siege were light: Americans, 20 killed and 56 wounded; French, 52 killed and 134 wounded; British, 156 killed and 326 wounded.

The surrender virtually ended the war in America, although minor skirmishes did continue. News of Cornwallis's defeat caused shock and consternation in London. A strong vote in Parliament to authorize the king to propose a peace conference left him with no recourse but to end the war. With the signing of the Treaty of Paris on September 3, 1783, Great Britain formally acknowledged the independence of the American colonies.

YORKTOWN BATTLEFIELD SITE

Located at 1000 Colonial Parkway. The Yorktown Battlefield Site was established by an act of Congress in 1936. The area is administered by the National Park Service.

VISITOR INFORMATION

Maps and brochures are available at the visitor center, 1000 Colonial Parkway. A film describes the relevant political and military events of the Revolutionary War in this region of Virginia. Dioramas and exhibitions are also very informative. Store with books, souvenirs, and other products. Open 9 a.m. to 5 p.m. Hours vary by season. Closed major holidays. A self-guided audio tour is available to drive your vehicle around a seven-mile battlefield loop. Admission fee: adults $15, youth (under the age of 15) free. Annual pass, $45. A combination ticket can be purchased for both the Yorktown Battlefield Site and the Jamestown Settlement for $66 (adults). Phone: (757)-898-2410.

Driving Tour

Start at the visitor center.
Major points of interest:
Redoubt 9
Redoubt 10
Allied First Siege Line
Supply Depot Site
Moore House
Surrender Field
Allied Encampment
French Battery
End at Route 238, or return to the visitor center.

Washington and His Generals at Yorktown (detail) by Charles Willson Peale. Left to right: Marquis de Lafayette, General Benjamin Lincoln, General George Washington, Comte de Rochambeau, Marquis de Chastellux, Colonel Tench Tilghman.
(MARYLAND CENTER FOR HISTORY AND CULTURE)

ALLIED ENCAMPMENT

The road moving south from Surrender Field (past the intersection of Route 17) leads through the area of the American and French encampments. Markers indicate the headquarters of Rochambeau and Washington, where they planned joint military strategies with their generals and senior officers.

ALLIED FIRST SIEGE LINE

Allied engineers studied the layout of the British lines before planning their own defenses. The first siege line stretched from the York River southeast of Yorktown to Yorktown Creek. During the night of October 6, almost 1,500 men began constructing redoubts and digging a series of trenches. By the next evening the Allied troops and artillery pieces were in position.

FRENCH BATTERY

Sections of the gun platforms and magazines of the French Battery have been reconstructed. Eighteenth-century artillery pieces, including several cannon used during the siege of Yorktown, have been mounted here.

MOORE HOUSE

Usually closed. Occasionally, tours can be arranged at the Visitor Center. On October 17, 1781, Cornwallis sent George Washington a note proposing a ceasefire and a meeting of commissioners to draw up the terms of his surrender. The following day British officers Lieutenant Colonel Thomas Dundas and Major Alexander Ross met the Allied representatives Lieutenant Colonel John Laurens and Second Colonel Viscount de Noailles at the house of Augustine and Lucy Moore.

Negotiations continued late into the evening because of arguments over Article III, which denied the defeated army the right to march out in salute to the victor with flags unfurled and drums resounding. Laurens vehemently insisted that the rites of an honorable surrender should

Moore House, Yorktown Battlefield Site (NATIONAL PARK SERVICE)

not be granted because General Clinton had denied the Americans similar privileges when he captured Charleston in 1780. The British were forced to retract their demand.

The Articles of Capitulation were first sent to Yorktown, where they were signed by General Charles Cornwallis and Captain Thomas Symonds, the senior British naval officer. The document was then delivered to the Allies and signed by Washington, Rochambeau, and Admiral de Barras.

Visitors to the Moore House—the gambrel-roofed, wood-frame structure built around 1725—may view the **Surrender Room**. Since none of the original furniture has survived, the Yorktown Restoration Committee has furnished the room with a round mahogany drop-leaf Queen Anne table and Queen Anne cabriole-legged side chairs.

REDOUBTS 9 AND 10

On the night of October 14, 1781, these two redoubts were seized by the Allies. Soon afterward they began digging trenches to connect the redoubts with the second siege line. A battery was also erected. Several days later, after the Articles of Capitulation had been accepted and signed by the British commanders, the Allied leaders met in Redoubt 10 to affix their signatures to the document.

SUPPLY DEPOT SITE

A sign and large painting now mark the location of the small American arsenal established here during the Battle of Yorktown.

SURRENDER FIELD

On October 19, 1781, the surrender ceremonies were held in this large field. At noon the French and American troops formed two parallel lines facing each other and extending more than one mile. Two hours later, the British army marched out of the garrison at Yorktown to the tune "The World Turned Upside Down."

General Cornwallis, claiming illness, was represented by Brigadier General Charles O'Hara. He first tried to surrender to Rochambeau,

Surrender of Cornwallis by John Trumbull (US CAPITOL, OFFICE OF THE ARCHITECT CF THE CAPITOL)

who turned away. When O'Hara next began to present Cornwallis's sword to General Washington, Washington, already insulted, refused to accept the token of surrender from a subordinate officer and directed him to present it instead to Major General Benjamin Lincoln. Once the ritual had been accomplished, the sword was returned to O'Hara. The Redcoats then marched between the columns of Allied troops—the Americans to the east and the French to the west—to an open field, where they laid down their arms. Under militia guard, the British soldiers were taken away to prison camps in Virginia and Maryland.

YORKTOWN—"TOWN OF YORK"

The community of Yorktown, which was established in 1691, is located near the battlefield. Fine examples of Colonial architecture may still be seen.

ARCHER COTTAGE

Water Street near the corner of Read Street. Not open to the public. A modest structure was built here in the 1730s by local merchant Abraham Archer. One of his grandsons, who inherited the property, became a naval officer and later a county magistrate. After the devastating fire of 1818 (which leveled the entire section of the town along the waterfront), the present one-and-a-half-story cottage was rebuilt on the original stone foundations.

CUSTOM HOUSE

Corner of Main and Read Streets. Open June to mid-October, Sunday, 1 p.m. to 4 p.m. In 1721, a small frame dwelling and a two-story brick storehouse were built on this lot. From here Richard Ambler conducted his business—registering the goods of ships that anchored in the York River, collecting marine taxes levied by the Crown, and issuing sailing papers to itinerant seamen.

During the Revolutionary War the buildings were seized by the Virginia militia for use as barracks.

DIGGES HOUSE

Main and Read Streets. Not open to the public. An early owner of this house was Dudley Digges, who served in the House of Burgesses for twenty-five years before the Revolution. Along with Patrick Henry and Thomas Jefferson, he was a member of the Virginia Committee of Correspondence. After the war, he was selected as a member of the Virginia Council.

During the Yorktown campaign of 1781, British soldiers were quartered here, and several American cannonballs penetrated the outer walls.

GRACE CHURCH

115 Church Street. Services are available Sunday, 8:30 a.m. and 10:30 a.m. Service times are subject to change. Parish Hall is located at 111 Church Street. Open Monday through Thursday, 10 a.m. to 3 p.m. This Episcopal church was built of native marlstone in 1697. During the siege of Yorktown, the British ripped out the pews and converted the building into a powder magazine. Thomas Nelson Jr., a native of Yorktown and a signer of the Declaration of Independence, was buried in the churchyard.

NELSON HOUSE

Nelson and Main Streets. Informal tours can be obtained by calling (757) 898-2410. Hours depend on staffing availability. This impressive brick Georgian house was built in the 1740s by "Scotch Tom" Nelson and was later the home of his grandson Thomas Nelson Jr. (1738–1789), a burgess from York County, a delegate to the Continental Congress, a signer of the Declaration of Independence, and a commander of Virginia militia units during the Revolutionary War. Nelson is remembered for the generous use of his own money to pay public debts, which left him impoverished. It is believed that this dwelling served as Cornwallis's headquarters during the last days of the Yorktown siege. Several cannonballs that penetrated the eastern wall give graphic evidence of the severity of the Allied bombardment of Yorktown. During Lafayette's 1824 tour, he was given a reception here by local dignitaries.

Nelson House, Yorktown Battlefield Site (LIBRARY OF CONGRESS, PRINTS AND PHOTO-GRAPHS DIVISION)

SWAN TAVERN

Main Street between Ballard and Church Streets. Owned by the National Park Service. The tap room is open on Thursday and Friday evenings. The Swan Tavern opened for business in March 1722 with Robert Wills serving as innkeeper. Colonial travelers and townspeople gathered here for drink, food, and entertainment. On hearing news of the Boston Massacre in 1770, a band of angry men left the tavern and began harassing British soldiers.

In December 1863, the building was destroyed by fire and was not reconstructed until the late 1930s. Today exhibition rooms occupy the first floor of the building, once one of Virginia's most famous "Publick Houses."

VICTORY MONUMENT

Main Street off Comte de Grasse Street. Visitors to Yorktown may wish to end their tour at the Victory Monument. In 1881, the US Congress

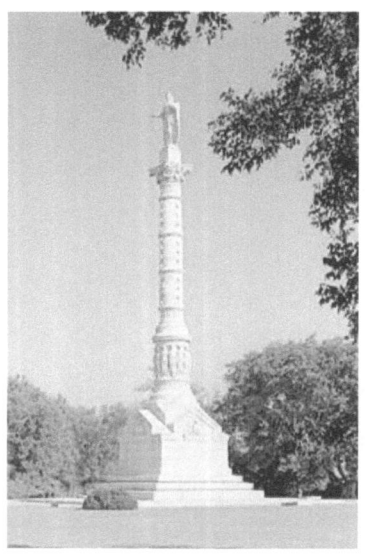

appropriated $100,000 for the erection of a monument commemorating the 100th anniversary of the Allied victory. The joint design of three artists—R. M. Hunt, J. A. Ward, and H. Van Brunt—was selected, and a cornerstone was laid on October 18, 1881, in the presence of President Chester A. Arthur and thousands of spectators.

Years later, after the ninety-five-foot shaft was completed, an allegorical figure, "Liberty Goddess," sculpted by John Quincy Adams Ward, was placed on top of the monument. The statue lost its head when struck by lightning in 1942, and a new figure was erected in 1956 (sculpted by Oskar J. W. Hansen).

Victory Monument, Yorktown Battlefield Site (LIBRARY OF CONGRESS, PRINTS AND PHOTOGRAPHS DIVISION)

RECOMMENDED SIDE TRIP
JAMESTOWN

Jamestown was the first permanent English settlement in North America. On May 13, 1607 (twenty-three years after the first attempted settlement at Roanoke Island and thirteen years before the Pilgrims landed at Plymouth), three ships carrying 104 passengers arrived at this site on the James River. The settlers were unprepared for what awaited them in the wilderness: starvation, disease, and hostile Indians. During the severe winter of 1609–1610 (the "Starving Time") 90 percent of the settlers died. The survivors were preparing to return to England when Lord De La Warr arrived (in June 1610) with men and supplies. From that moment Jamestown began to grow and prosper. Tobacco, which was first cultivated here in 1612 by John Rolfe, became an important export. After Rolfe married Pocahontas in 1614, relations with the Indians were greatly improved. In 1619, the first Africans were brought to the colony on a Dutch warship.

The British concept of representative government was transplanted to Jamestown. When the first legislature of the colony convened here in 1619, Jamestown became the seat of government of Virginia.

In 1676, many persons openly opposed the policies of the royal governor, and Nathaniel Bacon organized an armed revolt. The rebels attacked and burned Jamestown, which they considered the stronghold of oppression. Although the town was partially rebuilt, it began to decline after the government moved to Williamsburg in 1699.

On July 6, 1781, near Green Spring Plantation on the Williamsburg-Jamestown road, troops under the command of General Anthony Wayne made a valiant stand against Cornwallis's army. Lafayette sent a detachment to aid Wayne, but the Patriots were outnumbered and forced to withdraw. Almost 140 Patriots (out of 800 engaged in the battle) were casualties.

HISTORIC JAMESTOWN (JAMESTOWNE) COLONIAL PARK
1368 Colonial Parkway. Open daily, 9 a.m. to 5 p.m. Hours may vary by season. Tickets can be purchased through the Historic Jamestown Visitor Center. Preservation Virginia property tickets for adults $15, youth (6–17)

$5, children (under 5) free. National Park Service property tickets for adults $15, children (under 15) free. Other combination tickets are available. Closed Thanksgiving, December 25, and January 1. Phone: (757) 229-1733.

House of Burgesses Monument

On July 30, 1619, the first representative assembly in the New World met in a little cedar frame church here to discuss matters of importance to the colony. The monument lists the names of those first burgesses.

Hunt Memorial

Erected to the memory of Reverend Robert Hunt, the first minister of Jamestown, the monument features a plaque depicting in relief one of the settlement's early communion services.

Memorial Cross

During the terrible winter of 1609–1610 more than 400 colonists died from hunger and disease. This impressive stone cross marks the area where they were laid to rest.

New Towne Area and Museum

Still standing here are the foundations of several seventeenth-century dwellings. Near the river once stood the first State House, which served the colony from 1641 to 1656. Visit the Voorhees Archaeological Museum.

Old Church Tower

This brick tower is all that remains of the church built here in 1639. After 1750, the building fell into ruin. Behind the tower is Memorial Church, erected in 1907 by the National Society of the Colonial Dames of America.

Pocahontas Statue

This statue by sculptor William Ordway Partridge represents Pocahontas (c. 1595–1617), daughter of the Indian chief Powhatan. She is remembered for saving the life of Captain John Smith, who had been captured by the Indians and sentenced to death. In 1613, Pocahontas was seized by a party of settlers so that an exchange might be arranged for English prisoners held by her father. While in Jamestown, she was converted to Christianity and baptized Rebecca. John Rolfe fell in love with the Indian princess and, after marriage, took her (in 1616) to England, where she fell ill and died.

John Smith Statue

Designed by William Couper, the statue overlooking the James River honors one of the significant figures of Jamestown's early history, Captain John Smith (c. 1579–1631). A member of the governing council of the settlement, he established trade with the Indians, and his resourceful leadership helped see the colony through periods of intense suffering.

Tercentenary Monument

Rising 103 feet above its base, this granite shaft was erected in 1907 to commemorate the 300th anniversary of the settlement of Jamestown.

JAMESTOWN SETTLEMENT

2110 Jamestown Road, Route 31 South. Visitor center / museum complex open daily, 9 a.m. to 5 p.m. Hours may vary by season. Admission fee to Jamestown Settlement: adults $20, youth (6–12) $10, children (under 5) free. **America's Historic Triangle** *tickets to Colonial Williamsburg, Jamestown Settlement, and Yorktown Battlefield Site: adults $123, youth (6–15) $55. Virginia American Heritage Annual Pass: adults $34, youth (6–17) $17, children (under 5) free. Closed Thanksgiving, December 25, January 1. Phone: (757) 253-4838.* This site was constructed in 1957 for the celebration of the 350th anniversary of the settling of Jamestown. Maintained by the Commonwealth of Virginia, the Jamestown Settlement schedules numerous historical reenactments throughout the year.

The Gallery of States

The flags of the fifty states are displayed in this plaza.

James Fort

James Fort is a full-scale reconstruction of the triangular palisade built by the settlers in 1607 for protection against the Indians and animals.

Within the walls are the guardhouse, storehouse, church, and more than a dozen small log cabins.

Jamestown Exhibition Galleries

Refurbished in 2019, these galleries (30,000 square feet) feature technology-driven exhibits of the region's history and culture. Of special interest are documentary films, interactive maps, and theme-based dioramas. Trace the social, economic, and political development of the Virginia colony that seventeenth-century Englishmen sought to transplant to the new world, despite encountering enormous challenges.

Powhatan's Lodge

This small structure is a reconstruction of a typical ceremonial hut used by the Indians who lived in this region.

Three Colonial Ships

Full-scale replicas of the three vessels that carried the first settlers to Jamestown are located at the dock facing James Fort—the *Susan Constant* (76 feet, 100 tons), the *Godspeed* (50 feet, 40 tons), and the *Discovery* (38 feet, 20 tons).

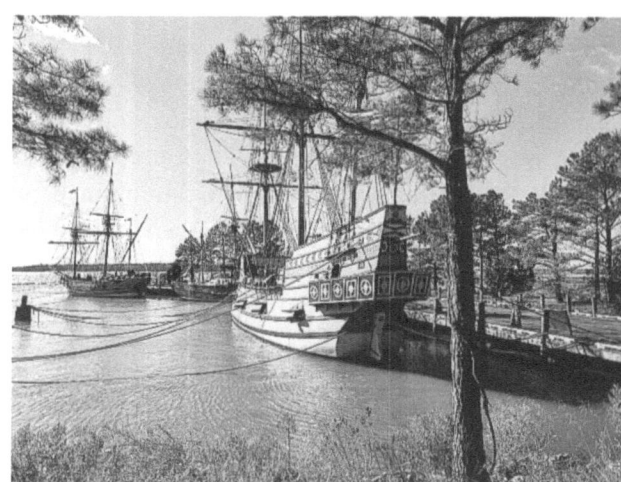

Full-scale replicas of Colonial ships, Jamestown Settlement (LIBRARY OF CONGRESS, PRINTS AND PHOTOGRAPHS DIVISION)

Richmond

REVOLUTIONARY WAR HISTORY

In 1737, William Byrd II (1674–1744), a wealthy landowner and member of the House of Burgesses, laid plans for a settlement on the James River. Incorporated as a town in 1742, Richmond had over 2,000 inhabitants by the time of the Revolutionary War. In March 1775, after Royal Governor Dunmore dissolved the House of Burgesses in Williamsburg because of their advocacy of a boycott on British goods, the legislators came to Richmond to meet at St. John's Episcopal Church. The approximately 120 members included George Washington, Thomas Jefferson, Patrick Henry, Benjamin Harrison, George Wythe, and George Mason. The following July, after the battles of Lexington and Concord, a group of Patriots held meetings in Richmond, where they appointed a Committee of Safety and prepared a plan for bolstering the strength of the colony's militia units.

In 1780, the capital of Virginia was moved from Williamsburg to Richmond, which then became a bustling town and important port. British soldiers, under Major John G. Simcoe, soon began a series of devastating raids on the area that lasted nearly a year. In January 1781, the forces of the turncoat Benedict Arnold burned and plundered Richmond for three days. The Patriot militia was unable to repel these attacks, and Washington, at the urging of Governor Thomas Jefferson, finally sent reinforcements. On April 29, Lafayette arrived leading regiments of the New England and New Jersey Light Infantry. They pushed back the British assault and remained in Richmond for a month before marching northward to meet other units of the Continental Army.

On June 16, Charles Cornwallis's troops, moving from the Carolinas toward Yorktown, passed through Richmond.

In June 1788, five years after the formal end of the Revolutionary War, the Virginia Convention held to ratify the Federal Constitution convened in this city. Despite the persuasive arguments of Patrick Henry to reject the document, the delegates voted to unite with the other states under a federated government.

VISITOR INFORMATION

Richmond Region Visitor Center, 200 North Arthur Ashe Boulevard; (804) 340-1515

Virginia Welcome Center, 1500 East Main Street; (800) 847-4882

Virginia Chamber of Commerce, 919 East Main Street; (804) 644-1607

PUBLIC TRANSPORTATION The Greater Richmond Transit Company provides local bus service. For information and schedules, call (804) 358-4782 or visit www.ridegrtc.com.

TAXI SERVICE Rainbow Taxicab, (804) 484-4300; Henrico Express Cab, (804) 867-3232; Veterans Cab, (804) 275-5542

WALKING AND DRIVING TOURS Most of Richmond's important sites can be seen in two downtown walking tours and a drive (traveling west) along Monument Avenue. ("NR" signifies an important non-Revolutionary site; "P" indicates a historic Colonial house that is now a private residence.)

Walking Tour A

Area bounded by Leigh Street on the north, Main Street on the south, 13th Street on the east, and 5th Street on the west.

Start at the Capitol.

Capitol

Capitol Square

St. Paul's Church (NR)

Lee House (NR)

John Marshall House

Valentine Museum (NR)

Museum of the Confederacy (NR)

End near 12th and Clay Streets.

Walking Tour B

Area bounded by Broad Street on the north, Main Street on the south, 25th Street on the east, and 18th Street on the west.

Start at Broad Street near 24th Street.

St. John's Church

Craig House (P)

Poe Museum (NR)

End at Main Street near 19th Street.

Driving Tour

Start at Capitol Square and drive west on Grace Street until you come to Lombardy Street. Turn left and proceed to Monument Avenue, where you turn right. When you reach Westmoreland Avenue—several blocks past Boulevard—turn left and travel until you come to Cary Street Road. Stop at the appropriate sites along this route.

Hopkins-Call House (P)

Monument Avenue (NR)

Virginia Museum of History and Culture

Wilton

End on Wilton Road, off Cary Street Road.

COLONIAL AND REVOLUTIONARY WAR SITES
THE CAPITOL

1000 Bank Street. Open Monday through Saturday, 9 a.m. to 5 p.m.; Sunday, 1 p.m. to 5 p.m. Tours begin at 9 a.m. by appointment; the last tour begins at 4 p.m. Free. Phone: (804) 698-1788. Built in the late 1780s, the central structure of the Capitol is an adaptation by Thomas Jefferson of the Maison Carrée in Nimes, France. The Virginia Assembly convened in the old hall of the House of Delegates from 1788 until 1906. A major structural change of the building was made in 1906 when wings for the two houses of the legislature (the Senate and the House of Delegates) were added.

In the Rotunda stands the famous marble statue of George Washington by Jean-Antoine Houdon (1741–1828). In 1784, the Virginia

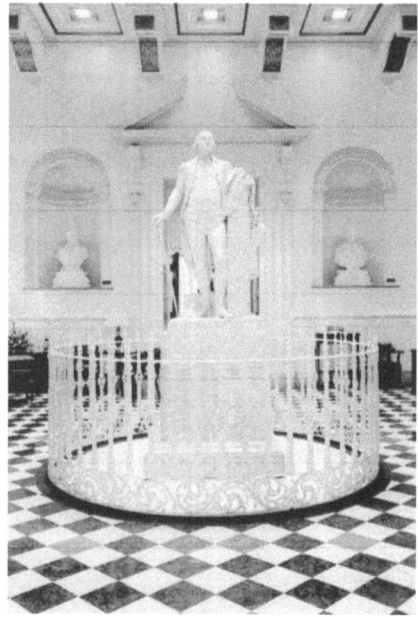

Houdon statue of George Washington, Capitol Rotunda, Richmond (LIBRARY OF CONGRESS, PRINTS AND PHOTOGRAPHS DIVISION)

Assembly voted appropriations for a statue of General Washington. Thomas Jefferson, then in France, commissioned the renowned sculptor Houdon for the project. In October 1785, he arrived at Mount Vernon, where he made a model of his distinguished subject, then fifty-three years old and four years away from the presidency.

In the niches around the Capitol Rotunda are marble busts of Lafayette and several Virginia-born presidents. A significant event in the history of the Capitol occurred in 1807 when Aaron Burr (1756–1836), vice president under Thomas Jefferson from 1800 to 1804, was tried and acquitted of treason during a six-month trial here.

CAPITOL SQUARE

At 9th Street to Governor Street and Broad Street to Bank Street stands Richmond's celebrated sculpture of Virginia's Revolutionary leaders. At the center of the sixty-foot-high monument is an equestrian statue of George Washington flanked by the figures of Jefferson, Henry, Marshall, Lewis, and Nelson. The sculptor was Thomas Crawford. The cornerstone was laid February 22, 1850, in the presence of President Zachary Taylor and other distinguished guests.

JOHN MARSHALL HOUSE

818 East Marshall Street at 9th Street. Open Friday through Sunday, 10 a.m. to 5 p.m. Hours and fees may vary. Closed major holidays. General admission $15, children (under 6) free, seniors $12, students $10, military $12. Phone:

(804) 648-1889. This brick dwelling was built in 1790 by John Marshall (1755–1835), who served as chief justice of the US Supreme Court from 1801 to 1835. The small wing and three porches were added around 1805. The house, which contains the original floors and paneling, is furnished with many original pieces and family portraits.

Born in a log cabin on the Virginia frontier, Marshall left home as a young man to fight in the American Revolution. After serving in the Patriot forces that defeated the British at Great Bridge, Virginia (in December 1775), he was commissioned a lieutenant in the Third Virginia Continentals. By the time he retired from military service in 1781, he had seen action at Germantown, Monmouth, and Stony Point. Marshall then served as a member of the Virginia Assembly (1782–1797), a member of the US House of Representatives (1799–1800), and secretary of state (1800–1801) in the cabinet of President John Adams.

During his tenure as chief justice of the Supreme Court, he made landmark decisions in the case of *Marbury vs. Madison* (1803), which established the power of the Court to overrule acts of Congress or state legislatures that it considered unconstitutional, and in *Gibbons vs. Ogden* (1824), which confirmed congressional control of interstate and foreign commerce. Marshall also presided over the 1807 trial of Aaron Burr in Richmond.

ST. JOHN'S EPISCOPAL CHURCH

2401 East Broad Street. Visitor center open Monday, 9:30 a.m. to 4 p.m.; Thursday, 11:30 a.m. to 4 p.m.; Friday through Saturday, 9:30 a.m. to 4 p.m.; Sunday, 12:30 p.m. to 4 p.m. Daily tour general admission $12, youth $9. Reenactment general admission $15, children (under 12) $12. Phone: (804) 649-7938. On March 23, 1775, Patrick Henry's famous words rang out here: "I know not what course others may take, but as for me, give me Liberty or give me Death!" His speech urging the colony into a state of defiance fell on the sympathetic ears of the Virginia burgesses, who were convening here because Royal Governor Dunmore had dissolved the legislature, depriving Virginians of their rights to representative government.

St. John's Episcopal Church, Richmond
(LIBRARY OF CONGRESS, PRINTS AND PHOTO-
GRAPHS DIVISION)

St. John's was the only church in Richmond until 1814. Built in 1740–1741, the original rectangular structure (which measured twenty-five feet by forty feet) was enlarged in 1772 by an extension on the north side and the addition of a belfry. A chancel and vestry room were added to the south end in 1880, giving the church the cross shape it now has.

Visitors to St. John's may see the pew Patrick Henry stood in while delivering his speech and the baptismal font used to baptize the Indian princess Pocahontas. (It was moved here from a church that had fallen into disrepair and is no longer in use.)

In the churchyard are buried two distinguished men of the Revolutionary period: George Wythe (1726–1806), a member of the Virginia House of Burgesses and a signer of the Declaration of Independence, and Dr. James McClury (1746–1823), a physician who served during the War of Independence as director general of Virginia's military hospitals.

VIRGINIA MUSEUM OF HISTORY AND CULTURE

428 North Arthur Ashe Boulevard. Open daily, 10 a.m. to 5 p.m. Closed major holidays. Adults $12, youth (6–17) $8, children (under 5) free, seniors, military, and students $10. Phone: (804) 340-1800. Formerly known as the Virginia Historical Society, this institution houses an expansive collection of art, documents, artifacts, weapons, memorabilia, and furniture. Exhibitions explore Virginia's past. Of special interest to Revolutionary War buffs is a sword presented to Peter Francisco, the "giant" who ferociously attacked the British at the Guilford Courthouse (March 15, 1781). Charles Willson Peale's portrait of Lafayette and Thomas Sully's painting of Pocahontas are also displayed here.

WILTON

215 South Wilton Road. Open Wednesday through Saturday, 10 a.m to 4 p.m. Closed major holidays. Adults $10, seniors and students $8, children (under 6) free. Tours available. Phone: (804) 282-5936. Wilton was built in the 1750s by William Randolph III, a member of the Virginia House of Burgesses. The design of this imposing Georgian mansion is attributed to Richard Taliaferro, leading Williamsburg architect. The structure was originally located on a bluff overlooking the James River roughly ten miles east of Richmond. Here Randolph and his wife, Anne (sister of Benjamin Harrison of Berkeley, a signer of the Declaration of Independence), lived with their seven children.

Thomas Jefferson (whose mother was a Randolph) and George Washington were frequent visitors to Wilton. On May 15, 1781, General Lafayette made his headquarters here but hastily departed five days later when Cornwallis crossed the James River in pursuit of him.

After Randolph's death, the estate passed through the hands of many owners. In 1933, the Colonial Dames of America, rescuing the mansion from destruction, moved it to its present site in Richmond.

IMPORTANT COLONIAL HOUSES

AMPTHILL

211 Ampthill Road. Not open to the public. Built by Henry Cary, the architect of many of Williamsburg's public buildings, this elegant mansion was begun in 1732. The central court and dependencies were added in 1750. The house was moved to Richmond from its site in Cumberland County in 1929.

CRAIG HOUSE

1812 East Grace Street. Not open to the public. Built between 1784 and 1787, this large two-story structure was the home of Adam Craig, clerk of the Richmond Hustings Court, the Henrico County Court, and the General Court.

SITE OF HOPKINS-CALL HOUSE

217 West Grace Street. Demolished in 2024. The dwelling that once stood here was probably built in the mid-eighteenth century and was owned by

John Hopkins (commissioner of loans), who rented it to Jean-Auguste-Marie Chevallie, an agent of Pierre-Augustin Caron de Beaumarchais, the famous French playwright who furnished arms to the Patriots in 1776–1777 and who was instrumental in gaining French aid for the American colonies. The house was sold in 1798 to Daniel Call, a distinguished lawyer and brother-in-law of John Marshall.

NON-REVOLUTIONARY SITES OF INTEREST
AMERICAN CIVIL WAR MUSEUM
480 Tredegar Street. Open daily, 10 a.m. to 5 p.m. Closed major holidays. Fees: $10 to $19. Phone: (804) 649-1861. This museum has an excellent collection of artifacts, weapons, memorabilia, documents, and art associated with Civil War themes—social, economic, military, and political.

HOLLYWOOD CEMETERY
412 South Cherry Street. Open daily, 8 a.m. to 5 p.m. Phone: (804) 648-8501. Many distinguished leaders, including Presidents James Monroe (1758–1831) and John Tyler (1790–1862) and Confederate President Jefferson Davis (1808–1889), are interred here.

LEE HOUSE
707 East Franklin Street. Currently closed to the public. Built in 1844, this three-story Greek Revival house was used by Confederate General Robert E. Lee in 1864–1865 during his Virginia campaign.

MONUMENT AVENUE
A boulevard running east–west from the terminus of Franklin Street at Lombardy Street to Horsepen Road. For generations, five imposing monuments lined this avenue. They were removed in 2020–2021 due to political and legal issues.

J. E. B. Stuart Monument Site
Monument Avenue and Lombardy Street. The equestrian statue of the Confederate cavalry general was designed by Fred Moynihan and dedicated in May 1907.

Robert E. Lee Monument Site

Monument Avenue and Allen Avenue. The statue of Robert E. Lee mounted on his beloved horse Traveller was the first to be raised on Monument Avenue. The work was executed by French sculptor Jean Antonin Mercié, and the unveiling took place on May 29, 1890.

Jefferson Davis Monument Site

Monument Avenue and Davis Avenue. Honoring the president of the Confederacy, this monument consisted of a statue of Davis at the foot of a soaring column topped by a female figure. A semicircular colonnade surrounded the shaft. The monument was designed by Edward Valentine and unveiled in June 1907.

Thomas J. "Stonewall" Jackson Monument Site

Monument Avenue and Boulevard. This equestrian statue, which honored Confederate General "Stonewall" Jackson, was sculpted by F. William Sievers and dedicated in October 1919.

Matthew F. Maury Monument Site

Monument Avenue and Belmont Avenue. Designed by F. William Sievers and dedicated in November 1929, this monument paid tribute to Matthew F. Maury, commodore of the Confederate navy and an important oceanographer.

POE MUSEUM

1914 East Main Street. Open Tuesday through Saturday, 10 a.m. to 5 p.m.; Sunday, 11 a.m. to 5 p.m. Adults $12, youth (7–17) $6, seniors and military $10, children (under 6) free. Phone: (804) 648-5523. The Poe Museum—which displays memorabilia, including many of the writer's possessions—occupies Richmond's oldest house, a rough stone structure built in the late 1680s. Although Edgar Allan Poe (1809–1849) lived and worked in the area for twenty-six years, he did not reside in this building. (He lived at various locations: Main and 5th Streets, Main and 13th Streets, and 5th and Leigh Streets.) The adjacent carriage house of the Poe Museum exhibits drawings based on his well-known stories and poems.

RICHMOND NATIONAL BATTLEFIELD SITE
3215 East Broad Street (on US 60), in Chimborazo Park. Open Wednesday through Sunday, 9 a.m. to 4:30 p.m. Closed Thanksgiving, December 25, and January 1. Free. Two of the seven attempts to capture Richmond during the Civil War took place in this area. Visitors who follow the foot trail will see breastworks, fortifications, and other landmarks that remain from General George McClellan's attack (1862) and General Ulysses S. Grant's campaign (1864–1865).

ST. PAUL'S CHURCH
815 East Grace Street. Open Monday through Thursday, 9 a.m. to 4 p.m.; Sunday, 9 a.m. to 12 p.m. Phone: (804) 643-3589. Confederate President Jefferson Davis and General Robert E. Lee frequently worshipped at this church (built in 1845). It was during services on Sunday morning, April 2, 1865, that President Davis received the tersely worded message from General Lee that the government must evacuate Richmond and that supplies must be destroyed so they would not fall into the hands of the approaching Union army.

VALENTINE MUSEUM COMPLEX
1015 East Clay Street. Open Tuesday through Wednesday, 10 a.m. to 5 p.m.; Thursday, 10 a.m. to 7 p.m.; Friday through Sunday, 10 a.m. to 5 p.m. Closed major holidays. Adults $12, children free, seniors $10, students free, groups of 10 or more $10, members free. Phone: (804) 649-0711.

Bransford-Cecil House
Built in 1840, it was moved from 5th Street to this site in 1954.

Valentine Studio
Originally the studio of sculptor Edward Valentine (1838–1930).

Wickham-Valentine House
The main structure of this three-building complex is a restored Federal-style mansion. It was built in 1812 by John Wickham (1763–1839), one of the lawyers who successfully defended Aaron Burr in 1807 against charges of treason. On the death of the last occupant, Mann Valentine, in 1891, the house was converted into a museum.

RECOMMENDED SIDE TRIPS
HANOVER
From Richmond, take US 301 North for around 18 miles.

HANOVER COURTHOUSE
7505 Library Drive. In this T-shaped brick courthouse (built in the 1730s), twenty-seven-year-old Patrick Henry won fame in December 1763 in a case referred to as "The Parson's Cause." Henry argued that his client, Parson James Maury, and other clergymen had been harmed by the Two Penny Acts, which forced ministers to accept paper money of the colony (valued around £133) in lieu of their usual annual salary of 16,000 pounds of tobacco (£400 market value). While tobacco was a convenient medium of exchange, especially in England, the paper money forced on the clergymen was a depreciated currency and almost worthless outside the colonies. After hearing Henry's arguments, the jury decided that Reverend Maury was entitled to damages.

HANOVER TAVERN
13181 Hanover Courthouse Road, US 301. Open Wednesday through Sunday, 11 a.m. to 7 p.m. Phone: (804) 537-5050. This structure (built around 1723) was acquired in 1760 by Patrick Henry's father-in-law, John Shelton. Henry and his wife, Sarah, lived in the family quarters of the tavern for several years in the 1760s, and it is known that he frequently tended bar here. Cornwallis occupied rooms at the tavern briefly during the Virginia campaign of 1781. Today the building is used as a dinner theater.

PATRICK HENRY BIRTHPLACE SITE
Located at the intersection of Studley and Williamsville Roads. A stone marker records the location of Henry's birthplace.

PLANTATION HOUSES

Berkeley
12602 Harrison Landing Road. Open daily, 9:30 a.m. to 5 p.m. Adults $18, children (under 6) free, youth (7–17) $7.50, seniors $16.50. Annual pass for

adults $50, children $25. Phone: (804) 829-6018. After plundering Richmond (January 1781), the traitor Benedict Arnold—then a general in the British army—led his soldiers toward Portsmouth. Pausing at Berkeley Plantation, they killed cattle, destroyed furnishings, and harassed neighbors. Nearby, they set ablaze warehouses filled with tobacco and ransacked a foundry while seizing munitions.

Berkeley was the home of two presidents: William Henry Harrison (1773–1841), ninth president of the United States, and his grandson, Benjamin Harrison (1833–1901), twenty-third president. Berkeley has the distinction of having been visited by every president from Washington to Buchanan (from 1789 to 1861). During the Civil War, the mansion was seized by General McClellan for his headquarters.

Shirley

501 Shirley Plantation Road. Group tours available through appointment only. Adult groups $25. Student groups $25, students $18. Phone: (804) 829-5121. This Georgian mansion—a three-story brick building with colonnaded porticoes—was begun around 1723 by Edward Hill III, whose daughter Elizabeth married John Carter, son of wealthy and powerful Virginian Robert "King" Carter. Another member of the family who resided here was Anne Hill Carter, who married Henry ("Light-Horse Harry") Lee, the Revolutionary War cavalry officer. The Carters entertained George Washington, Thomas Jefferson, and many other distinguished leaders at Shirley.

Charlottesville

REVOLUTIONARY WAR HISTORY

When Cornwallis invaded Virginia in 1781, members of the Virginia government considered it unsafe to remain in Richmond. On May 10, 1781, the legislature adjourned, with plans to meet again in Charlottesville on May 24. Governor Thomas Jefferson returned to his home in Monticello near Charlottesville, and forty members of the legislature took quarters in the town. (Among them were four signers of the Declaration of Independence—Richard Henry Lee, Thomas Nelson Jr., Benjamin Harrison, and Thomas Jefferson.)

Hoping to capture these prominent leaders, Cornwallis dispatched to the area Lieutenant Colonel Banastre Tarleton with a troop of 180 cavalry and 70 infantrymen. On the morning of June 3, they left the British encampment on the North Anna River (around twenty miles north of Richmond) and advanced swiftly toward Charlottesville. At 11 p.m. they reached Louisa Courthouse, fifty-five miles from their destination. Tarleton's forces rested there for three hours and then pushed on again through the night. As they passed the Cuckoo Tavern twelve miles down the road, Jack Jouett—a captain in the Virginia Militia and a resident of Charlottesville—observed the enemy's movements. He was spending the night at the tavern, according to some sources, after courting a local maiden. Aware of the imminent peril to the legislators in Charlottesville, he quickly saddled his mare and rode furiously toward the town. Hoping to reach his destination in time to sound the alarm, he followed an old Indian path known only to local residents.

At dawn he reached Milton (a short distance from Monticello) and roused the local inhabitants, shouting, "The British are coming!"

Gasping for air, he arrived ten minutes later at Monticello, awakening Jefferson and his household. After informing the governor of Tarleton's approach, Jouett rode into Charlottesville spreading the news.

When Tarleton reached the town, he could see that his mission had failed. Seven legislators who had delayed their flight were the only prisoners he could take. Enraged, he ordered his men to destroy property and seize military supplies. To the dismay of the citizens, the Redcoats carried the county records to the courthouse green to destroy them in a fierce conflagration. On June 5, after receiving information that the local militia was organizing, Tarleton, with his prisoners, withdrew toward Tidewater.

Jouett's gallant action received official recognition from the Virginia Assembly in December 1786 when the grateful legislators introduced a resolution commending his courage and presented him with a handsome sword and a pair of pistols.

MONTICELLO

The mansion is located at 931 Thomas Jefferson Parkway. Parking is available at 1050 Monticello Loop. Open daily, 8:30 a.m. to 5:30 p.m. Closed Thanksgiving and Christmas. Hours may vary by season. Purchase tickets at the Rubenstein Visitor Center, which also offers a film and exhibits. Adults $22, children (under 5) free, youth (5–11) $2, adolescents (12–17) $8. Various tours are available for additional fees and are listed on the Monticello website: www .monticello.org. Phone: (434) 984-9800.

Monticello was the home of Thomas Jefferson (1743–1826), author of the Declaration of Independence (1776), governor of Virginia (1779–1781), minister to France (1785–1789), secretary of state (1790–1793), and third president of the United States (1800–1808).

Because Jefferson's estate is located on the crest of one of the highest hills in the area, he named it Monticello, which means "little mountain" in Italian. He planned and supervised every stage of the building of his mansion. Construction began around 1769, but because of numerous alterations in the design, the house was not completed until 1809. Crowned by an octagonal dome, the structure is symmetrical in appearance and has two long L-shaped balustraded terraces with pavilions at each end. These terraces served a special purpose—to roof and conceal small outbuildings such as a kitchen, dairy, smokehouse, and laundry. The small pavilion at the tip of the south terrace is known as the "Honeymoon Cottage" because in January 1772, with the main house still incomplete, Jefferson brought his bride, Martha Wayles Skelton, to live here.

When Jack Jouett brought news on the morning of June 4, 1781, of the approach of Tarleton's troops, Jefferson sent his wife and children fourteen miles away to Enniscorthy, the home of his friend Colonel Coles. While two trusted slaves concealed valu-

Thomas Jefferson by Mather Brown (NATIONAL PORTRAIT GALLERY, SMITHSONIAN INSTITUTION)

ables under the floor of the portico at Monticello, Jefferson climbed a nearby hill with a telescope to view the terrain. Seeing the approach of the Redcoats, he swiftly departed to join his family. The property and the grounds received little damage at the hands of the British. Tarleton was so anxious to push on toward Charlottesville that he ordered his men to restrict their activity to raiding the wine cellar.

Although Jefferson's political career forced him to spend many years away from Monticello, he did retire here in 1809 after serving two terms as president.

In 1819, he encountered serious financial difficulties when a friend failed to cover a note Jefferson had endorsed. He was about to sell his lands when a sympathetic public rallied to his aid with voluntary contributions. One year after Jefferson's death, however, his heirs were forced to hold a public sale of furnishings. Two years later the estate was purchased for $7,000 by James T. Barclay, a Charlottesville apothecary. Monticello then passed through many hands until the Thomas Jefferson

Memorial Foundation purchased it in 1923 for $500,000. Various renovations were undertaken from 2017 to 2022.

The house holds many attractions for visitors. For some persons, the chief interest lies in the beautiful interior decoration and furnishings; for others, the focus of attention is Jefferson's inventions.

He designed the timekeeping system in the **Entrance Hall**. The cannonballs on the right wall mark the day of the week and the time of day as they descend, controlled by eight weights (located on the left wall), which also regulate the gong on the roof. The busts near the entrance are of Voltaire, Anne Robert Jacques Turgot, and Alexander Hamilton.

The **Parlor** doors, operated by metal drums connected by a chain, open simultaneously when either is moved. The floor of this elegant room—squares of cherry with beechwood border—is thought to be the first parquet in America. The Louis XVI furniture is similar to the pieces Jefferson brought to Monticello from Paris in the late 1780s; the harpsichord was made around 1800 in London for his daughter Martha.

Monticello, Charlottesville (CAROL M. HIGHSMITH ARCHIVE, LIBRARY OF CONGRESS)

On each side of the **Dining Room** mantel (which is decorated with unusual Wedgwood medallions) are dumbwaiters used to bring wine bottles from the cellar. The fine ormolu and marble clock on the mantel was purchased in France. The Chippendale dining table is believed to have been a wedding gift from George Wythe, Jefferson's friend and former law teacher. Prominent figures such as James Monroe and James Madison were entertained here. During his visit to Monticello in November 1824, Lafayette dined here after being reunited with his friend in an emotional ceremony on the south lawn.

All the furniture in the **Master Bedroom** is original to the house. The unit comprising the chair, the table, and the long bench—forming a kind of chaise longue—was arranged by Jefferson in his later years so that he could write in a comfortable position. The profile of Jefferson was executed by artist Amos Doolittle, and the plaster bust of John Adams is a copy of the work by J. B. Binon. Jefferson died in this bed at the age of eighty-three on July 4, 1826—fifty years after signing the Declaration of Independence. He is buried in the family cemetery on the grounds of his beloved Monticello.

OTHER SITES NEAR MONTICELLO
ASH LAWN / HIGHLAND

2050 James Monroe Parkway. Open daily, 9:30 a.m. to 4:30 p.m. Adults $18, children (under 6) free, youth (7–17) $13. Closed Thanksgiving, December 24, December 25, January 1. Phone: (434) 293-8000. Ash Lawn, also known as Highland, was the home of James Monroe (1758–1831). As a young man, he fought in the American Revolution and was a delegate to the Continental Congress. Later, he served as United States senator (1790–1794), minister to France (1794–1796), and governor of Virginia (1799–1802), and he participated in the negotiations with France that led to the Louisiana Purchase (1802–1803). Monroe became secretary of state (1811–1817) under James Madison and served two terms as the fifth president of the United States (1817–1825).

This house, built in 1799, was designed by Thomas Jefferson, Monroe's friend and neighbor. The Monroes maintained this residence for twenty-one years before moving into their large home, "Oak Hill,"

James Monroe, engraving by Goodman and Piggot after C. B. King (NATIONAL PORTRAIT GALLERY, SMITHSONIAN INSTITUTION)

near Leesburg, Virginia. In the 1860s, several structural modifications were made by the new owners of Ash Lawn.

Many of the furnishings here once belonged to President Monroe: the Hepplewhite table and the Duncan Phyfe chairs in the dining room; the hand-carved mahogany bed and the medicine chest in the master bedroom; and the sofa and chairs (a gift of Napoleon I) in the drawing room.

In the boxwood gardens stands a marble statue of Monroe, unveiled here on the 100th anniversary of his death. The sculptor was Attilio Piccirilli.

MICHIE TAVERN

683 Thomas Jefferson Parkway. Open for lunch, 11:30 a.m. to 3 p.m. The General Store open Monday through Friday, 11 a.m. to 4 p.m.; Saturday through Sunday, 11 a.m. to 5 p.m. 1784 Pub and restaurant open Thursday through Saturday, 3:30 p.m. to 7 p.m. Phone: (434) 977-1234. The oldest section of this elongated building (which dates from 1735) was originally located on the Back Mountain Road in North Albemarle and served as Patrick Henry's boyhood home. In 1746, the house was sold to John Michie, who enlarged it and established a tavern. Michie, a Scotsman, had come to Virginia after taking part in an abortive uprising against the Crown. He had been captured and sentenced to take part in a lottery to decide his fate—execution or exile. The condemned prisoners drew from a bag containing black and white beans. Those who drew black were shot; Michie drew white and was forced to bid farewell forever to his native land.

Many of the furnishings here are original. Among the rare items are a dulcimer, a "banister" chair, a clock with painted eagle and stars, a Chippendale blanket chest, and several hurricane sconces.

The taproom is the only original Colonial bar in existence in Virginia. According to tradition, the "round dance," or waltz, was introduced to America in the upstairs ballroom. (Some local historians speculate that it was introduced by Jefferson's daughter, who had learned the dance in France.)

In 1927, Michie Tavern was moved to its present site and refurbished.

DOWNTOWN CHARLOTTESVILLE
GEORGE ROGERS CLARK MEMORIAL MONUMENT
Located in Monument Square, bounded by University and Jefferson Park Avenues. Originally located at West Main Street near 12th Street. Born near Charlottesville, George Rogers Clark (1752–1818), brother of explorer William Clark, fought the British and Indian forces in the Northwest Territory. In 1778, he persuaded Governor Patrick Henry to send an expedition against the British-held settlements of Kaskaskia, Cahokia, and Vincennes. Because of his success as a military strategist, he was sometimes called the "George Washington of the West." The monument was created by sculptor Robert Ingersoll Aitken and was unveiled on January 6, 1922.

LEWIS AND CLARK MEMORIAL MONUMENT
In Starr Hill at the intersection of West Main Street and Ridge–McIntire Road. This memorial honors the Lewis and Clark Expedition (1803–1806) that was approved by President Jefferson and the US Congress. The purpose was to discover a route to the Pacific and to survey the lands newly acquired by the Louisiana Purchase.

The sculptor, Charles Keck, depicts Meriwether Lewis (1774–1809) and William Clark (1770–1838)—both born near Charlottesville—and the young Indian woman who aided the expedition, Sacajawea. The monument was dedicated on November 21, 1919.

UNIVERSITY OF VIRGINIA
West Main Street. Free tours of the campus—offered Friday, Saturday, and Sunday—can be scheduled through the Office of Undergraduate Admissions. Phone: (434) 982-3200. Founded by Thomas Jefferson in 1819, the

university opened for instruction in 1825. Jefferson also designed the eight original buildings on campus, including the imposing Rotunda at the north end of the quadrangle. Edgar Allan Poe and Woodrow Wilson were among the many distinguished persons who, as students, resided in the West Range. In 2025, more than 26,000 students were enrolled here.

Fredericksburg

REVOLUTIONARY WAR HISTORY

In 1727, the Virginia Assembly directed that fifty acres of "lease-land" be developed here as the town of Fredericksburg (named for Frederick Louis, Prince of Wales and son of George II). Throughout the eighteenth century, Fredericksburg was an important port and center of political activity.

The town is well known for its association with George Washington and his family. He spent his boyhood at Ferry Farm across the Rappahannock River and attended school in Fredericksburg. For many years his mother and sister continued to reside here.

Six generals who fought in the Revolutionary War came from Fredericksburg and vicinity: George Washington, Hugh Mercer, George Weedon, William Woodford, Gustavus Wallace, and Thomas Posey. John Paul Jones, the Revolutionary War naval hero, also lived for a time in Fredericksburg.

During the Revolution, arms for the Patriot cause were manufactured at the gunnery located here. Many important leaders of the period visited the town, including Thomas Jefferson, Patrick Henry, George Mason, George Wythe, and Edmund Pendleton. In 1780, Nathanael Greene passed through Fredericksburg on his way to assume command of the Southern forces. After the British surrender at Yorktown in October 1781, citizens of surrounding farms and villages converged on the town for a great celebration honoring the visiting heroes of the battle. A gala Peace Ball held at the Rising Sun Tavern was the high point of the festivities.

Lafayette was a guest at the homes of several of Fredericksburg's leading citizens while he was touring the United States in 1824. During the official welcoming ceremonies the town's children—dressed in red, white, and blue—sang the *Marseillaise*. In the evening Lafayette attended a ball given in his honor.

Fredericksburg justly takes pride in the role it played in our nation's early history.

VISITOR INFORMATION

Visitors to Fredericksburg can get information from the **Fredericksburg Visitor Center**, 601 Caroline Street; (540) 373-1776. Open daily, 9 a.m. to 4 p.m. First Fridays open 9 a.m. to 8 p.m. Closed major holidays.

Fredericksburg Chamber of Commerce, 1701 Fall Hill Avenue; (540) 373-9400

GUIDED TOURS Trolley Tours of Fredericksburg, (540) 273-0867

PUBLIC TRANSPORTATION Fredericksburg Regional Transit, 1400 Emancipation Highway. For bus schedules and routes, call (540) 372-1222 or visit www.fredericksburgva.gov.

TAXI SERVICE Global Cab VA LLC, (540) 657-2227; Gary's Taxi, (540) 891-6555

TOURS After stopping at the visitor center, if you wish to start your tour at Kenmore, travel down Princess Anne Street until you come to Lewis Street; turn right and proceed to Washington Avenue. (Some sightseers may wish to start at the Mary Washington House.)

Driving Tour

Start on Washington Avenue between Lewis and Fauquier Streets.

Kenmore

Mary Washington Monument

Mary Washington House

Rising Sun Tavern

Mercer Apothecary Shop

Monroe Museum

Masonic Lodge

End on Princess Anne Street near Hanover Street.

COLONIAL AND REVOLUTIONARY WAR SITES
KENMORE

1201 Washington Avenue. Open March to October, Monday through Saturday, 10 a.m. to 5 p.m.; Sunday, 12 p.m. to 5 p.m. November to December, Monday through Saturday, 10 a.m. to 4 p.m.; Sunday, 12 p.m. to 4 p.m. Adults $12, children (under 5) free, students $6, military $11. Phone: (540) 373-3381. Construction of this brick Georgian mansion began in 1752, when Fielding Lewis married his nineteen-year-old sweetheart, Betty (the sister of George Washington). The estate, originally called Millbank, extended for 861 acres.

Fielding Lewis was elected to the Virginia House of Burgesses in 1760 and served on several of its important committees during the following years. But he is perhaps best remembered as a great Revolutionary War Patriot. He supervised the Fredericksburg Gunnery, which manufactured armaments for the Continental Army, and, when public

Kenmore, Fredericksburg (LIBRARY OF CONGRESS, PRINTS AND PHOTOGRAPHS DIVISION)

funds were exhausted, used his own money to keep it in operation. As chairman of the Virginia Committee of Safety, Lewis undertook various responsibilities: He was in charge of the purchase and the fitting of military vessels; he helped secure provisions for the troops; and he traveled extensively throughout the colony to inspire young men to bear arms for the Patriot cause.

During the Revolutionary period, many famous leaders visited the Lewis home—Thomas Jefferson, Patrick Henry, George Mason, the Marquis de Lafayette, the Comte de Rochambeau, and John Paul Jones.

George Washington's diaries record almost forty visits here. He frequently stopped on his way to Williamsburg, the Colonial capital, where he was a member of the House of Burgesses. During the week of celebration after the Battle of Yorktown, almost all the prominent officers were received by the Lewis family. Washington and Lafayette were overnight guests on that occasion.

Fielding Lewis died in 1781, leaving a debt amounting to $7,000 and a mortgage on Millbank, causing his wife to dismiss many servants and sell parcels of the estate. After Mrs. Lewis's death in 1797, the property was sold, passing through many hands until the first decade of the nineteenth century, when it came into the possession of the Gordon family, who changed the name to Kenmore.

The house, designed by architect John Ariss, is noted for its exquisite interior. The outstanding feature of the **Dining Room** is the elaborate relief decoration on the ceiling—a rayed circle, perhaps a sun-god image, is surrounded by circular motifs and rosettes. The Queen Anne Virginia dining table stands in front of the fireplace, with its carved mantel bearing the Washington crest, the "Swan and Crown." On the Chippendale-design mahogany huntboard stands a silver triple urn that belonged to the Lewises. China and glassware once owned by the Lewis and Washington families are also on display.

The elegant **Great Room** is distinguished by its relief overmantel, which depicts a scene from Aesop's fable "The Fox and the Crow." This overmantel is thought to have been designed by George Washington (from European style books) and executed by two Hessian prisoners. A

The Great Room, Kenmore, Fredericksburg (LIBRARY OF CONGRESS, PRINTS AND PHOTO-
GRAPHS DIVISION)

fine fire screen, once the possession of Lord Botetourt, a royal governor
of Virginia, adorns the hearth. Nearby, John Wollaston's portraits of
Betty and Fielding Lewis show the dignity and character of his subjects.
The great room's extraordinary carved ceiling combines circular motifs
with stylized leaf designs. Although the Chippendale sofa and chairs are
not original to the house, they are similar to those used here.

The **Library** has walls painted Pompeian red. Inspired by the fres-
coes in the ruins of Pompeii (which had been discovered in 1748), this
color became popular in the last half of the eighteenth century. The
highboy—a Philadelphia piece (c. 1750)—is unusually attractive; it has
a broken-arch pediment and finials.

Betty Lewis's bed (a four-poster Chippendale with blue-and-white
hangings), her desk, and her trunk may be seen in the **Master Bedroom**.

MASONIC LODGE

803 Princess Anne Street. Phone: (540) 373-5885. George Washington was initiated into Fredericksburg Lodge Number 4 on November 4, 1752, and was raised to a Master Mason on August 4, 1753. His initiation took place in Market Hall, which stood at the corner of Market Alley and Caroline Street. The building was torn down in 1812, and a new Masonic Hall was erected the next year here on Princess Anne Street.

Fielding Lewis, Washington's brother-in-law (the owner of Kenmore), was also a member of this Lodge. Lafayette was made an honorary member in 1824.

On display here are the Bible on which Washington was sworn, a lock of his hair, and a portrait of him by Gilbert Stuart.

MERCER APOTHECARY SHOP

1020 Caroline Street. Open March 1 to April 30, Sunday 12 p.m. to 4 p.m.; Monday, Wednesday through Saturday, 10 a.m. to 4 p.m. May 1 to October 31, Sunday, 12 p.m. to 4 p.m.; Monday through Saturday, 10 a.m. to 4 p.m. November 1 to February 28, Sunday, 12 p.m. to 4 p.m.; Monday, Wednesday through Saturday, 11 a.m. to 4 p.m. Closed major holidays. Adults $10, children (under 6) free, youth (7–17) $5, seniors $8. Phone: (540) 373-3362. In this small building, Dr. Hugh Mercer (1725–1777) practiced medicine and operated an apothecary shop.

Born in Aberdeen, Scotland, he took a degree in medicine from the University of Aberdeen in 1744. Two years later, he left his homeland to settle in Pennsylvania. While serving as a captain (1754–1756) under General Edward Braddock during the French and Indian War, he met young Colonel George Washington—the beginning of a close and lasting friendship. After the war, at Washington's suggestion, he settled in Fredericksburg, opened this shop, and married Isabel Gordon, sister-in-law of George Weedon (innkeeper of the Rising Sun Tavern). Washington, a frequent visitor here, sometimes used the library and office.

When the Revolutionary War began, Mercer closed his office and enlisted for military service. Because of his military experience, he was commissioned a brigadier general in the Continental Army in June 1776. Seven months later, he was killed in the Battle of Princeton.

This shop—where medicines were mixed and sold—displays pill-boxes, bottles, pap boats, carboys, and accessories such as mortars, pestles, lancets, and bleeding pans. When the shop was restored around 1930, a false partition was discovered, behind which were stored many eighteenth-century bottles. (It is believed that Mercer had concealed his equipment before going off to war.) In the adjoining room, Dr. Mercer examined patients and performed surgery.

MONROE MUSEUM

908 Charles Street. Open Monday through Saturday, 10 a.m. to 4 p.m.; Sunday, 1 p.m. to 4 p.m. Adults $6, children $2, seniors $5. Closed Thanksgiving, December 24, December 25, and Easter. Phone: (540) 654-1043. Dating from 1758, this brick building has changed little since James Monroe (1758–1831) practiced law here from 1786 to 1789. He shared a practice with Robert Brooke and Bushrod Washington. (Brooke became a governor of the state; Washington was later appointed an associate justice of the US Supreme Court.) Monroe served as the first district attorney of this section of Virginia, and his political career culminated in his inauguration as the fifth president of the United States in 1817.

This museum now contains personal belongings of the Monroe family: the desk on which President Monroe prepared the message to Congress (December 1823) setting forth principles of the so-called Monroe Doctrine; a six-and-a-half-pound umbrella with whalebone ribs presented to him in 1824 by the City of Boston; a bust of Lafayette, which the Frenchman presented to Monroe during his visit to the United States in 1824; and several pieces of furniture used in the new White House. (The White House was burned by the British during the War of 1812; it was reconstructed several years later, in time for Monroe's occupancy in 1817.)

The gown Mrs. Monroe wore at the court of Napoleon is on display, along with a topaz necklace and matching earrings.

The library and archive contain 26,000 original documents, over 3,000 rare books, and hundreds of Monroe's personal letters.

RISING SUN TAVERN

1304 Caroline Street. Open March 1 to April 30, Sunday, 12 p.m. to 4 p.m.; Monday, Wednesday through Saturday, 10 a.m. to 4 p.m. May 1 to October 31, Sunday, 12 p.m. to 4 p.m.; Monday through Saturday, 10 a.m. to 4 p.m. November 1 to February 28, Sunday, 12 p.m. to 4 p.m.; Monday, Wednesday through Saturday, 11 a.m. to 4 p.m. Tours are available. Adults $10, children (under 5) free, youth (6–17) $5, seniors $8, military $8. Phone: (540) 371-1494. Located on the route between Alexandria and Williamsburg, this popular tavern was built around 1760 by George Washington's youngest brother, Charles.

As hostilities with England intensified in the 1770s, the innkeeper of the Rising Sun, George Weedon, was accused by Loyalists of "blowing the seeds of sedition." He not only wrote numerous fiery letters entreating his friends to defy the authority of the Crown but also urged open rebellion in 1775, when Royal Governor Dunmore seized the

Rising Sun Tavern, Interior Room, Fredericksburg (LIBRARY OF CONGRESS, PRINTS AND PHOTOGRAPHS DIVISION)

powder stored in the magazine at Williamsburg. The irate citizens of Fredericksburg who met here to organize a march to the capital were spurred to action by Weedon's impassioned words.

Among the Patriots who gathered here during the Revolution to discuss the course of affairs were George Washington, Patrick Henry, Thomas Jefferson, George Mason, John Marshall, and Hugh Mercer. In 1777, a committee of burgesses (Jefferson, Mason, Wythe, and Pendleton) met at the tavern to draft the "Bill for Establishing Religious Freedom" for presentation to the Virginia Assembly.

After affairs of state were attended to, the distinguished guests turned to relaxation. Describing an evening at the gaming table, George Washington wrote in his diary, "Evening at the Rising Sun . . . Lost money as usual. The boys at Fredericksburg are too smart for me." After the Yorktown victory, Fredericksburg enjoyed a week of festivities. Visitors flocked to the town, and a Peace Ball was held in the assembly room of the tavern on November 11, 1781. Among the guests were George Washington and his mother, Colonel James Monroe, General Anthony Wayne, and the Marquis de Lafayette. The Rising Sun Tavern is a two-and-a-half-story frame building with a steep gabled roof, narrow dormer windows, and built-in end chimneys. The eighteenth-century furnishings and accessories are of English and American origin.

MARY WASHINGTON HOUSE

1200 Charles Street at Lewis Street. Open March 1 to April 30, Sunday 12 p.m. to 4 p.m.; Monday, Wednesday through Saturday, 10 a.m. to 4 p.m. May 1 to October 31, Sunday, 12 p.m. to 4 p.m.; Monday, Wednesday through Saturday, 10 a.m. to 4 p.m. November 1 to February 28, Sunday, 12 p.m. to 4 p.m.; Monday, Wednesday through Saturday, 11 a.m. to 4 p.m. Adults $10, children (under 5) free, youth (6–17) $5, seniors $8, AAA members $8, military $8. Phone: (540) 373-1569. George Washington's mother, who had resided for three decades at Ferry Farm across the Rappahannock River, moved to Fredericksburg in 1772 when her son purchased this small frame house for her. (The north wing is a later addition.) With her housekeeper, Polly Skelton, and two Black servants, Mrs. Washington continued to live here for sixteen years—tending her garden, entertaining

Mary Washington House, Fredericksburg (ALPER)

guests, and exchanging visits with her daughter, Betty Lewis (who resided at a nearby estate, Kenmore).

After the British defeat at Yorktown, the triumphant Washington came to visit his mother and sister. During the same week, Lafayette arrived and blushed to hear Mrs. Washington remark, "It is strange to think of you as a general; you look just a boy."

Washington's last visit here was on April 12, 1789, when he knelt beside his mother's sickbed to receive her blessing before journeying to New York to be inaugurated as the first US president. She died four months later. The house contains many possessions of the Washington family, including a mirror, a waistcoat, several kitchen implements, and a Wedgwood china set. Among the noteworthy antiques are a secretary-desk, a pencil-post bed, an Oriental birdcage, and French silver chests.

In the garden, the same boxwoods Mary Washington planted two centuries ago may still be seen.

MARY WASHINGTON MONUMENT

1500 Washington Avenue. Open daily, dawn to dusk. Free. A large granite shaft marks the grave of George Washington's mother, Mary Ball Washington (1708–1789). When she died in 1789, her coffin was carried from the church on the shoulders of six Kenmore servants and laid to rest here (on land originally part of the Kenmore estate).

In 1832, Silas E. Burroughs, a wealthy New York merchant, donated money for the building of a monument to Mary Washington. The following year President Andrew Jackson laid the cornerstone, but work was halted when Burroughs went bankrupt.

During the Civil War the half-completed monument was scarred by shells and defaced by vandals.

Enthusiasm for a new monument was generated in 1890, and money was successfully raised by various organizations. In 1894, the ruined monument was removed and a shaft was erected. On May 10, crowds swarmed the streets and bands played as President Grover Cleveland and several congressmen arrived in Fredericksburg for the dedication ceremonies. They reviewed a parade of marching Masons, fire companies, and military units before delivering appropriate speeches. The monument was then dedicated by the Grand Master of Masons of Virginia.

In the evening President Cleveland visited the Mary Washington House to meet descendants of the Washington and Ball families. That night an elaborate reception was held in his honor at the Opera House.

IMPORTANT COLONIAL HOUSES

DICK HOUSE

Princess Anne Street between Amelia and Lewis Streets. Not open to the public. The original structure on this site was built in the early 1750s. Charles Dick, the owner, was in partnership with Fielding Lewis at the gunnery, which manufactured armaments for the Patriot forces.

JOHN PAUL JONES HOUSE

501 Caroline Street. Not open to the public. This dwelling was purchased in 1752 by John Paul Jones's older brother, William Paul. (John Paul Jones added the name "Jones" in 1775 to disguise his identity after he was involved in a murder in the West Indies.) This is the one house in America that the seafaring Jones considered his home. Scottish-born John Paul Jones (1747–1792) entered the newly established Continental Navy in 1775. The next year, while commanding the sloop *Providence*, he captured sixteen British ships. Promoted to commodore, Jones was placed in command of a fleet of five vessels. He named his flagship the *Bonhomme Richard* in honor of the character created by Benjamin Franklin in *Poor Richard's Almanack*. On the night of September 23, 1779, the fleet encountered a convoy of merchant ships accompanied by two men-of-war, the *Countess of Scarborough* and the *Serapis*. The *Countess* was captured by the American vessels, and Jones's flagship attacked the *Serapis*, forcing it to surrender.

MORTIMER HOUSE

213 Caroline Street. Not open to the public. This two-story house (built in 1755) was the home of Dr. Charles Mortimer, Mary Washington's physician and the first mayor of Fredericksburg. Many distinguished men were guests here: Washington, Lafayette, Rochambeau, and Henry Lee. Architectural alterations were made in the twentieth century.

WEEDON HOUSE ("SENTRY BOX")

133 Caroline Street. Not open to the public. General George Weedon (who commanded the Virginia troops during Yorktown) and his wife, Isabella, lived here after the Revolutionary War. Weedon hosted the family of General Hugh Mercer after the general's death at the Battle of Princeton. Mercer's children inherited this property. The name "Sentry Box" was adopted by Weedon as a whimsical reference to his war service. The tradition that the house was used as a lookout during three wars is erroneous.

NON-REVOLUTIONARY SITES OF INTEREST
FREDERICKSBURG AND SPOTSYLVANIA NATIONAL MILITARY PARK

This park consists of four battlefields covering 3,600 acres. The four Civil War battles that occurred here were the Battle of Fredericksburg, the Battle of Chancellorsville, the Battle of the Wilderness, and the Battle of Spotsylvania Courthouse.

VISITOR INFORMATION

The Information Center, 1013 Lafayette Boulevard, Fredericksburg, distributes maps for self-guided tours. Hours vary by season. Phone: (540) 693-3200. Narrative markers and monuments on each of the battlefields relate the events and identify the siege lines. Sunken Road Walking Tour available on weekends, 10:30 a.m. and 2 p.m.

Another information center for the Chancellorsville Battlefield site is located at 9001 Plank Road, Spotsylvania. Open daily 9 a.m. to 5 p.m. Hours vary by season. Phone: (540) 693-3200.

Battle of Fredericksburg (December 13, 1862)

General Ambrose Burnside moved his divisions along the north side of the Rappahannock River (opposite Fredericksburg) and delayed bringing up pontoon bridges, thereby preventing him from crossing to the south bank and occupying a strategic position. This provided time for Generals Robert E. Lee, Stonewall Jackson, and James Longstreet to prepare a strong defense. Union troops finally crossed the river, but they were unable to sustain an assault against the Confederate defenses. They lost more than 12,000 soldiers—a serious defeat for the North.

Battle of Chancellorsville (May 2–4, 1863)

Through a series of brilliant maneuvers, Robert E. Lee and Stonewall Jackson routed the Union forces under the command of Joseph Hooker at Chancellorsville (located roughly ten miles west of Fredericksburg).

Battle of the Wilderness (May–June 1864)

The Confederate forces of Robert E. Lee and the Union army under Ulysses S. Grant attacked and counterattacked in a series of inconclusive battles in an area of dense forest around eleven miles west of Fredericksburg. Losses were extremely high on both sides.

Battle of Spotsylvania Courthouse (May 8–19, 1864)

The fiercest fighting of the Wilderness campaign took place at Spotsylvania Courthouse, where Grant hammered away at Confederate lines.

On May 12, the Union army attacked the center (the "Bloody Angle") of the Confederate line and was repulsed in a serious setback. In June, the armies moved south toward Richmond, where Grant launched another unsuccessful assault and was finally forced to withdraw.

RECOMMENDED SIDE TRIP
WAKEFIELD (GEORGE WASHINGTON'S BIRTHPLACE)

1732 Popes Creek Road. Open daily, 9 a.m. to 5 p.m. Closed major holidays. Free. Phone: (804) 224-1732.

George Washington's great-grandfather John Washington reached Virginia in 1657 on an English merchant ship. During a violent storm the vessel, which was attempting to sail up the Potomac River, floundered and ran aground. John Washington, second officer, decided to remain in the New World. When he married Anne Pope two years later, his bride's father presented him with land on Mattox Creek (near Wakefield) as a wedding gift. John attained influence and respect in the community: He was elected vestryman of the church and in 1662 was appointed justice of Westmoreland County Court.

His son, Lawrence, served in the Virginia Militia and, at the age of twenty-five, was elected to the House of Burgesses. In 1690, he married Mildred Warner, daughter of a prominent planter. Their son, Augustine, born in 1694, was destined to become the father of our country's first president.

Augustine Washington married Jane Butler in 1715 and bought 150 acres here on Popes Creek (which flows into the Potomac a half mile away). Augustine, who had attended school in England, held several responsible positions: justice of Westmoreland County Court, sheriff of Westmoreland County, and captain in the militia. He also was co-owner of two iron furnaces. On his property at Popes Creek, he built a fine brick house (1724–1726). The family had lived here only three years when Jane fell ill and died, leaving Augustine to care for their three children. On March 6, 1731, he married a second time—to Mary Ball of Lancaster County, an orphan who had been living in the house of her guardian, George Eskridge. On February 22, 1732 (February 11, Old Style Calendar), their first son, George, was born here. He spent the first three years of his life at Wakefield until the family moved to a plantation fifty miles up the Potomac (now called Mount Vernon). The Popes Creek house passed to George's older half brother, Augustine Jr. When George was six years old, his father purchased 288 acres at Ferry Farm near Fredericksburg and relocated there.

WASHINGTON FAMILY CEMETERY
Buried here are generations of the Washington family, including George Washington's great-grandfather (John), grandfather (Lawrence), and father (Augustine). The large tombstones were erected in 1930 by the Wakefield National Memorial Association.

KITCHEN OUTBUILDING
This outbuilding was reconstructed in the 1930s on its original foundations. The east room now contains cooking utensils and furniture of the early eighteenth century. The west room is used as a museum to exhibit Colonial artifacts uncovered in the area and to present displays relating the early history of the Washington family.

Washington Family Cemetery, Wakefield (ALPER)

MEMORIAL HOUSE (WAKEFIELD MANSION)

The Washington house at Popes Creek (sometimes referred to as Wakefield Mansion) burned to the ground on Christmas Day 1779, probably as the result of sparks emitted from the chimney, which set the roof on fire. Since no reliable information exists about the exact location and appearance of the house, this building—constructed in 1930–1931—represents a typical plantation house of the Colonial period. The bricks were handmade of native clay. Memorial House is today furnished with eighteenth-century antiques. The only piece of furniture surviving from the original dwelling is a tilt-top table that was salvaged after the 1799 fire.

SITE OF BUILDING "X"

During excavations conducted on this site between 1930 and 1936, a brick foundation almost seventy feet long was unearthed. It was named Building "X" because little was known about its origin and history. The excavation was reopened in 2022, and advanced archaeological techniques revealed that this site represents a substantial eighteenth-century house—possibly owned by Augustine Washington Jr. or his son William.

WASHINGTON BIRTHPLACE MONUMENT

The United States War Department erected this granite shaft in 1896 near the foundations of the house in which George Washington is believed to have been born. In 1930, the monument, weighing almost fifty tons, was moved to its present location. It is modeled to the scale of one-tenth of the Washington Monument (completed in 1884) in the District of Columbia.

Alexandria

REVOLUTIONARY WAR HISTORY

In 1732, a group of merchants decided to create a port at West Point—at the junction of the Potomac River and Hunting Creek—in order to facilitate the export of Virginia tobacco to the European market. A community sprang up around the warehouses and docks and grew rapidly into a town, which in 1748 was incorporated. It was named Alexandria for John Alexander, wealthy owner of large tracts of land in the area.

Surveyor John West Jr. and his young assistant George Washington were commissioned to survey the land and lay out a formal street plan with eighty-four half-acre lots. Among the first purchasers of these lots were Lawrence Washington, William Ramsay, and John Carlyle.

Alexandria became a bustling port and, with the construction of more houses and commercial buildings, developed into a flourishing cosmopolitan city.

In early July 1774, after the British Parliament had passed legislation closing the Port of Boston to commerce, the Patriots of Alexandria assembled at the courthouse. Fiery speeches protested the act, and the citizens decided to offer aid to the Bostonians. George Mason, a trustee of Alexandria, led the opposition against the repressive policies of the Crown. He also drafted several important documents defining the rights of the colonists. During the Revolutionary War, recruits from this area—forming the core of the Fairfax County militia—distinguished themselves in the Virginia campaign.

VISITOR INFORMATION

The Alexandria Tourist Council, 221 King Street in the historic **Ramsay House**, provides information, maps, and parking passes. Open daily September through April, 10 a.m. to 5 p.m.; May through August, 10 a.m. to 6 p.m. Phone: (703) 838-5005.

TOURS Several tours are offered, including the Alexandria Colonial Tour and the Alexandria History Tour. Call (703) 519-1749 or visit www.visitalexandria.com/listings/alexandria-history-tours/.

PUBLIC TRANSPORTATION

DASH System, (703) 746-3274 or www.dashbus.com
Metrobus, (202) GO-METRO (202-466-3876)

TAXI SERVICE All American Limousine Service, (888) 583-0779; Go Green Cab, (703) 212-2000

It is recommended that visitors drive or take a bus to the Henry Lee House, the Friendship Fire Company, and the George Washington Masonic National Memorial. Most of the other sites can be seen by walking through the area bounded by Cameron Street on the north, Wolfe Street on the south, Union Street on the east, and Pitt Street on the west. ("P" indicates a historic Colonial house that is now a private residence.)

Walking Tour

Start at the corner of King and Fairfax Streets.

Ramsay House

Carlyle House

Gadsby's Tavern

Stabler-Leadbeater Apothecary Shop

Gilpin House (P)

Dick House (P)

Captains' Row (P)

Brown House (P)

Presbyterian Meeting House

End on Fairfax Street near Wolfe Street.

Colonial Alexandria was enriched by the presence of George Washington, its most prominent citizen. Washington was a trustee of the town, a parishioner of Christ Church, an organizer of the Friendship Fire Company, and the first Worshipful Master of the Lodge of Masons.

COLONIAL AND REVOLUTIONARY WAR SITES

CARLYLE HOUSE

121 North Fairfax Street. Open Monday through Tuesday, Thursday through Saturday, 10 a.m. to 4 p.m.; Sunday, 12 p.m. to 4 p.m. Adults $8, children (under 5) free, youth (6–17) $3. Closed Thanksgiving, December 24, December 25, and January 1. Phone: (703) 549-2997. This mansion, built in 1752, was the home of John Carlyle (a wealthy merchant and ship owner) and his wife, Sarah (daughter of Colonel William Fairfax, a close friend of George Washington).

Here in 1755 General Edward Braddock met with five royal governors—from Virginia, Massachusetts, New York, Maryland, and Pennsylvania—to discuss plans for waging and financing the French and Indian War. A letter was drawn up at that meeting urging the British government to tax the colonies. Carlyle was placed in charge of supplies for Braddock's expeditions.

The Carlyle house was the social center of Alexandria. It was always full of guests, among them Aaron Burr, John Marshall, John Paul Jones, George Washington, and Thomas Jefferson.

The house is noted for its exceptional woodwork, mantels, and paneling. The furnishings include Carlyle's writing desk and a small wooden coach that Washington had made for the Carlyle children.

CHRIST CHURCH

118 North Washington Street. Open Tuesday, 9 a.m. to 4 p.m.; Wednesday, 1 p.m. to 4 p.m.; Thursday and Friday, 9 a.m. to 4 p.m.; Saturday 12 p.m. to 4 p.m.; Sunday, 2 p.m. to 4:30 p.m. Closed March 30 to April 2, November 28 and November 29, December 26 and December 27. Phone: (703) 549-1450. This handsome brick church was designed by James Wren in the 1760s. He also lettered the tablets of the Lord's Prayer and the Ten Commandments that are located on either side of the pulpit.

For the maintenance of the church, the vestry levied a tithe on each parishioner, who paid taxes in tobacco. The first rector of Christ Church, the Reverend Townsend Dade (1765–1778), received an annual salary of roughly 17,000 pounds of tobacco.

George Washington served as a vestryman here, and he purchased pew number 60 for £36, 10s (an unusually high price). The pew is marked by a silver plate. The Reverend Thomas Davis, rector here from 1792 to 1806, officiated at Washington's funeral at Mount Vernon on December 18, 1799. The family Bible of Washington was presented to the parish in 1804 by George Washington Parke Custis, a grandson of Martha Washington.

Robert E. Lee, who was confirmed in this church, frequently worshipped here during his boyhood and in later years when he resided at Arlington. On Sunday, April 21, 1861—the day after he resigned his commission in the US Army—Lee came to this church to seek divine guidance for the onerous task that awaited him. Two days later, he assumed command of the Virginia military forces. A white tablet on the east wall honors the great general; his pew, number 46, bears a silver plaque.

FRIENDSHIP FIRE COMPANY / FRIENDSHIP FIREHOUSE MUSEUM

107 South Alfred Street. Open one Saturday each month, 11 a.m.–5 p.m. General admission $2, free for Alexandria residents. Phone: (703) 746-4311. The Friendship Fire Company was organized on August 5, 1774, as a volunteer firefighting unit. George Washington was one of its first members. While attending the Continental Congress in Philadelphia in 1775, he purchased a fire engine for £80 and had it transported to Alexandria by oxcart.

When the bell in the tower of the Friendship firehouse rang out a warning, local volunteers ran through the cobblestone streets to the firehouse, where they would break out the equipment (buckets, hooks, and ladders) and man the engine.

A replica of this company's first engine is on display here along with several other eighteenth- and nineteenth-century fire engines. Many paintings and prints depicting scenes from Washington's life adorn the wall. One engraving relates an often-repeated story about him: One day, as he was riding past a fire in Alexandria, he noticed that the fire engine was inadequately manned. Seeing several young gentlemen idly watching the struggling fire volunteers, Washington scolded them for not helping and, jumping from his horse, took charge of the engine himself.

The present brick fire station dates from the 1850s and has been renovated and enlarged.

GADSBY'S TAVERN

Museum located at 134 North Royal Street. Open mid-March to October 31, Monday through Tuesday, 1 p.m. to 5 p.m.; Thursday through Friday, 11 a.m. to 4 p.m.; Saturday, 11 a.m. to 5 p.m.; Sunday, 1 p.m. to 5 p.m. November 1– mid-March, Thursday through Friday, 11 a.m. to 4 p.m.; Saturday, 11 a.m.

Gadsby's Tavern, Alexandria (LIBRARY OF CONGRESS, PRINTS AND PHOTOGRAPHS DIVISION)

to 5 p.m.; Sunday, 1 p.m. to 5 p.m. Closed Thanksgiving, December 25, and January 1. Adults $5, youth (5–12) $3, children (under 5) and military, free. Phone: (703) 746-4242. Restaurant located at 138 North Royal Street. Open Wednesday through Saturday starting at 5:30 p.m. for dinner; Sunday, 11:30 a.m. to 2:30 p.m. Phone: (703) 548-1288.

The older section of this two-part structure was erected in 1752 and was known as City Tavern. Forty years later, John Wise, proprietor of the tavern, built the three-story brick addition as a hotel. In 1794, an Englishman, John Gadsby, purchased the property.

On at least two occasions, the young George Washington used this tavern as his headquarters. In 1754, when a lieutenant colonel in the Virginia Militia, he stayed here while recruiting and drilling two companies of Provincial troops to reinforce the Virginia frontier posts against attacks by the French and Indians. The following year, he again used the tavern as a base of operations while organizing militiamen to fight in General Edward Braddock's ill-fated campaign against Fort Duquesne. After the Revolutionary War, Washington was frequently feted here on his birthdays by the citizens of Alexandria. On his way from Mount Vernon to his presidential inauguration in New York in April 1789, he stopped at Gadsby's and was honored at a gala reception.

Several colorful events of the Revolutionary period took place here. A committee of Virginians (including George Washington and George Mason) met at the tavern in the summer of 1774 to prepare a preliminary draft of the "Fairfax County Resolves," which set forth demands for Colonial rights. Here, in 1777, John Paul Jones met Baron de Kalb and the Marquis de Lafayette, who both had recently arrived from Europe to fight for the Patriot cause. Many Revolutionary leaders—including Thomas Jefferson, Alexander Hamilton, Benjamin Franklin, and Henry Lee—rested and dined at this tavern.

In February 1779, the large **Ballroom** was the setting for a birthday celebration for George Washington. At this elegant ball and elaborate supper honoring him, many of his friends saw him for the last time. He died ten months later.

President John Adams attended a public dinner in the ballroom on June 11, 1800, and the newly elected president, Thomas Jefferson, was guest of honor at a banquet here on March 14, 1801. His arch rival, Aaron Burr, was present and, instead of paying tribute to Jefferson's victory, offered his toast to "the memory of our departed chief, George Washington." In 1824, a reception was given here for Lafayette, who was touring the United States.

In one of the upstairs **Bedrooms**, Anne Warren, celebrated English actress, died in 1808. While performing at Alexandria's new theater, Liberty Hall, she suddenly was seized by a severe pain and fell stricken. She was carried back to her room at the hotel, where, after suffering for many hours, she expired. Miss Warren was buried in the cemetery of Christ Church.

In 1816, a woman who occupied one of the third-floor bedrooms died under mysterious circumstances. One day an elegantly dressed woman accompanied by a young man arrived by ship in Alexandria. As no servants attended them, local observers became curious. On arriving at the hotel here, she collapsed, never to recover. Gossips speculated that the beautiful young lady was the daughter of a wealthy English family who, disobeying her parents' wishes, had married a man beneath her station. Fleeing to Virginia, she had become ill during the turbulent crossing. Her companion remained by her bedside throughout her illness, but when she died, he suddenly vanished. From that time on, the unidentified lady has been known as "The Female Stranger."

HENRY LEE HOUSE / LEE-FENDALL HOUSE MUSEUM AND GARDEN

614 Oronoco Street. Open Wednesday through Saturday, 10 a.m. to 4 p.m.; Sunday, 1 p.m. to 4 p.m. Adults $10, children $5. Closed May 28, June 19, Independence Day, September 3, October 15, November 12, Thanksgiving, December 25, and December 26. Guided tours are available. Phone: (703) 548-1789. This house was occupied by the widow and children of Virginia Patriot Henry ("Light-Horse Harry") Lee (1756–1818), the Revolutionary War cavalry officer who, after the war, was a member of Congress (1786–1788, 1799–1801) and governor of Virginia (1792–1795). He is also remembered for a phrase describing George Washington: "First in war, first in peace, and first in the hearts of his countrymen." Henry

Lee's son, Robert E. Lee (1807–1870), gained immortality as commander of the Confederate armies in the Civil War.

This house was built in 1795 by John Potts, who sold it four years later to William Fitzhugh, a cousin of Mrs. Lee. While the Fitzhughs were prospering in Alexandria, the Lees were suffering misfortune at Stratford. Drought and increasing debts caused the Lee estate to fall into disrepair, and Henry was imprisoned for debt in 1808. Two years later, Mrs. Lee moved her children and their belongings to a house in Alexandria on Cameron Street. (After Lee was released from prison, he went to Baltimore and later to the West Indies, where he spent his final years.)

Soon after her husband's death in 1818, Mrs. Lee rented this house on Oronoco Street from William Fitzhugh, who had moved to his Ravensworth estate (near Annandale). The Lee family resided here for seven years. This fifteen-room mansion has been restored and furnished with period pieces. Among the treasured items are an early nineteenth-century piano by Albrecht (Philadelphia), a green brocade Sheraton sofa, a Duncan Phyfe sewing table, a set of Davenport china, and a bedspread that belonged to Martha Washington. A letter from Lafayette, now framed and hanging in the hallway, is a memento of his visit to the Lees in 1824.

PRESBYTERIAN MEETING HOUSE

323 South Fairfax Street. Open Monday through Thursday, 9 a.m. to 4 p.m.; Friday, 9 a.m. to 12 p.m.; Sunday, 9 a.m. to 1 p.m. Sunday service at 8:30 a.m. and 11 a.m. Service times are subject to change. Phone: (703) 549-6670. This meetinghouse was completed in 1774 under the supervision of John Carlyle. In 1835, it was partially destroyed by fire but was rebuilt two years later. On December 14, 1799, when news arrived of George Washington's death, the meetinghouse bell—the only church bell in Alexandria—began to toll. Its knell was heard for four days until his body was laid to rest in the family vault at Mount Vernon. On December 29, special memorial services were held here under the auspices of the Washington Society and the local Masonic Lodge. Many prominent Alexandrians are buried in the churchyard: John Carlyle (commissary of Virginia forces under Braddock), Dr. James Craik (surgeon general of the Continental Army and Washington's personal physician), and Colonel Dennis Ramsay (an officer in the Continental Army, later a mayor of Alexandria and one of the pallbearers at Washington's funeral). Here also lie the remains of an unidentified Continental soldier—in the Tomb of the Unknown Soldier of the Revolutionary War.

RAMSAY HOUSE

Functions as the visitor center. 221 King Street. Open daily, September to April, 10 a.m. to 5 p.m.; May to August, 10 a.m. to 6 p.m. Closed Thanksgiving, December 25, and January 1. Phone: (703) 838-5005. This dwelling was built around 1749 by William Ramsay, one of Alexandria's most prominent citizens. During his long public career, he served as census taker, postmaster, member of the Committee of Safety, town trustee, and adjustor of weights and seals. He has the distinction of having been Alexandria's first and only lord mayor.

Ramsay married Anne McCarty, a cousin of George Washington. Mrs. Ramsay was devoted to the cause of improving the welfare of the orphaned children of Revolutionary War soldiers.

Some architectural historians believe the Ramsay House may have been built at Dumfries (roughly twenty-five miles away) and moved here by barge; others claim the structure has always stood on its present location. The present dwelling, however, is a reconstruction, not a restoration, as the house was almost totally destroyed by fire in 1942. Since Ramsay had a large family, it is probable that he resided elsewhere in Alexandria and merely used this small house as an office or warehouse.

After a fire, the renovated structure was used as a visitor center in 1956.

STABLER-LEADBEATER APOTHECARY MUSEUM

105–107 South Fairfax Street. Open spring to summer, Sunday through Monday, 1 p.m. to 5 p.m.; Wednesday through Friday, 11 a.m. to 4 p.m.; Saturday, 11 a.m. to 5 p.m. Fall to winter, Wednesday through Friday, 11 a.m. to 4 p.m.; Saturday, 11 a.m. to 5 p.m.; Sunday, 1 p.m. to 5 p.m. Closed Thanksgiving, December 25, and January 1. Self-guided adults $5, children (under 4) free, youth $3. Guided adults $8, children (under 4) free. Phone:

Stabler-Leadbeater Apothecary Museum, Alexandria (LIBRARY OF CONGRESS, PRINTS AND PHOTOGRAPHS DIVISION)

(703) 746-4554. In 1792, Edward Stabler opened an apothecary shop in this building, which for more than 140 years was a leading Alexandria establishment. Among the famous people who at one time patronized the shop were George Washington, Henry Lee, Daniel Webster, John C. Calhoun, and Robert E. Lee.

All the counters here are not only original but also in their original locations. Many examples of eighteenth-century apothecary equipment are on display: mortars, pestles, lancets, scales, and jars. Of special interest are the tall tapered bottles with twelve sides that were designed by Stabler in 1796, the cobalt blue poison bottles, and the nursing bottles with glass nipples. The large "show-globes" in the front windows were used to identify apothecary shops. (According to tradition, a globe would be filled with red liquid during an outbreak of contagious disease, thereby warning strangers not to remain in the town.)

The large clock in the rear of the shop has been here since 1792. The black chair is said to have been a favorite of Robert E. Lee's when he visited the shop. Local historians believe that Lee was in this apothecary in October 1859 visiting with the proprietor, Mr. Leadbeater, when Lieutenant J. E. B. Stuart delivered orders from General Winfield Scott instructing Lee to proceed to Harpers Ferry to take command of defenses during John Brown's raid.

Much treasured are the extant records here. The documents include a note written by Martha Washington in 1802 for a quart of castor oil, an order for paint from George Washington Parke Custis, and a note from Nellie Custis (Mrs. Lawrence Lewis) requesting borax and pills.

The shop was in continuous use until 1933, when it was purchased by the Landmarks Society.

GEORGE WASHINGTON MASONIC NATIONAL MEMORIAL

101 Callahan Drive. Open Monday and Thursday through Sunday, 9:30 a.m., 11 a.m., 12:30 p.m., 2 p.m., 3:30 p.m. Adults $20, children (under 12) free. Phone: (703) 683-2007. This monument was built as a memorial to George Washington, who served as the first Worshipful Master of Alexandria Lodge Number 22. The 333-foot tower was designed by architect Harvey Wiley Corbett, who is said to have modeled it after a temple in Alexandria, Egypt. Construction was begun in 1923 on Shuter's Hill, one of the sites originally proposed for the United States Capitol Building. On May 12, 1932, this impressive Masonic temple was dedicated during ceremonies attended by President Herbert Hoover.

Memorial Hall—with its magnificent coffered ceiling and imposing marble colonnade—is dominated by a seventeen-foot bronze statue of George Washington executed in 1950 by sculptor Bryant Baker of New York. The two large murals, painted by Allyn Cox, show Washington presiding at ceremonies for the laying of the Capitol cornerstone and attending Christ Church in Philadelphia. Several stained-glass windows depict scenes in the lives of Benjamin Franklin, Dr. Joseph Warren, and the Marquis de Lafayette.

Elevators moving along slanted shafts carry visitors to the seven floors above Memorial Hall. The main rooms are the **Washington Museum**, displaying memorabilia of the Washington family; the **Library** of 6,000 volumes, primarily devoted to subjects associated with the Masonic Fraternity; the **Grotto Room**, decorated with Persian architectural elements; the **Royal Arch Room**, featuring paintings illustrating scenes from the Old Testament; the **Cryptic Room**, simulating the interior of the crypt reportedly built under King Solomon's Temple; the **Knights Templar Chapel**, dominated by the stained-glass window depicting the Ascension of Christ; and the **Observation Area**, offering a panoramic view of Alexandria.

This temple—built with the contributions of more than 3 million Masons—is the national home of Freemasonry. Each Grand Lodge is an active member of the George Washington Masonic National Memorial Association, and any Masonic body or individual Mason may become an honorary life member by contributing to the endowment fund.

IMPORTANT COLONIAL HOUSES
CAPTAINS' ROW
100 block of Prince Street. Not open to the public. These charming eighteenth-century town houses were built by sea captains when Alexandria was a thriving port. According to local tradition, Hessian prisoners laid the cobblestones on this street.

Dr. James Craik, Surgeon General of the Continental Army, artist unknown (NATIONAL LIBRARY OF MEDICINE)

CRAIK HOUSE
210 Duke Street. Not open to the public. Built around 1790, this was the home and office of Dr. James Craik (1730–1814), surgeon general of the Continental Army and director of the hospital at Yorktown. As George Washington's attending physician, he was present at the president's deathbed.

DICK HOUSE
209 Prince Street. Not open to the public. This three-story town house was owned by Dr. Elisha Cullen Dick, a prominent physician and health officer of Alexan-

dria. He succeeded Washington as Worshipful Master of the Alexandria Lodge of Masons. He was summoned by Dr. Craik to Mount Vernon for consultation at Washington's deathbed. According to tradition, Dick stopped the hands of the bedroom clock at the moment of Washington's death.

FAWCETT HOUSE

517 Prince Street. Not open to the public. One of the oldest houses in the Alexandria area, this structure retains fine architectural elements of the eighteenth century.

GILPIN HOUSE

208 King Street. Not open to the public. Colonel George Gilpin, who had served as an aide to George Washington during the Revolutionary War, built this three-and-a-half-story brick house in 1798. Active in the affairs of Alexandria, Gilpin was judge of the Orphans' Court, director of the Potomac Navigation Company, and postmaster. He served as a pallbearer at Washington's funeral.

LAFAYETTE HOUSE

301 St. Asaph Street. Not open to the public. When Lafayette visited Alexandria in 1824, he was a guest at this fine town house, then owned by the Lawrison family.

RECOMMENDED SIDE TRIPS
ARLINGTON

In Virginia, Interstate 95 and US 1 lead to Arlington. From the District of Columbia, take the Arlington Memorial Bridge (near the Lincoln Memorial) across the Potomac River.

Arlington County was originally a part of the District of Columbia but was returned to Virginia in 1846. The area is heavily populated with government workers.

CUSTIS-LEE MANSION (ARLINGTON HOUSE)

Off Sherman Drive at the edge of Arlington National Cemetery. Open daily, 9:30 a.m. to 4:30 p.m. Closed Thanksgiving, December 25, and January 1. Free. This mansion was built between 1802 and 1817 by George Washington Parke Custis (Martha Washington's grandson). In 1831, his daughter Ann married Robert E. Lee (son of Henry Lee, the Revolutionary War cavalry officer), and in the succeeding thirty years they raised seven children here.

During the Civil War the Lees abandoned the mansion after removing most of the family possessions. It was occupied by Union soldiers because of its strategic position overlooking the capital. In 1865, when Mrs. Lee did not pay the property taxes, the estate was confiscated by the federal government. At that time, land was set aside for establishment of a national cemetery.

The mansion—with its imposing grand portico of eight massive Doric columns—is an outstanding example of Greek Revival architecture. The design is attributed to George Hadfield, an Englishman who supervised work on the Capitol Building. Congress authorized the restoration and refurnishing of the Custis-Lee Mansion in 1925. In front of the main portico is a granite monument marking the grave of Pierre Charles L'Enfant (1754–1825), an officer in the Continental Army who saw service at Valley Forge, Savannah, and Charleston. He later drew up plans for the layout of the city of Washington, DC.

ARLINGTON NATIONAL CEMETERY

Directly west of Memorial Bridge in Arlington, 1 Memorial Drive is the main entrance to the cemetery. Open daily, 8 a.m. to 5 p.m. Free. Phone: (877) 907-8585. The largest burial ground in the United States, Arlington National Cemetery is a semicircular tract of roughly 639 acres with almost 400,000 graves of military personnel and eligible dependents. Among the famous persons buried here are George Washington Parke Custis, William Jennings Bryan, William Howard Taft, Oliver Wendell Holmes, General John J. Pershing, John Foster Dulles, President John F. Kennedy, and Senator Robert Kennedy.

GUIDED TOUR

Since no automobiles are allowed in the cemetery, persons wishing to tour the area may take a guided tour by tram, which leaves from the visitor center on Arlington Ridge Road. Available daily, 8:30 a.m. to 4 p.m. Tours run every 20 minutes; tickets $22.50 (may be less with special offers). Or contact Viator Tours at (888) 651-9785.

The major monuments here include the Marine Corps War Memorial and the Tomb of the Unknown Soldier.

Marine Corps War Memorial (Iwo Jima Statue)

Arlington Boulevard near Arlington Ridge Road. This statue depicts the raising of the American flag on Mount Suribachi, Iwo Jima, on February 23, 1945.

In February 1945, after seventy-two days of bombing, the United States Marines stormed the island of Iwo Jima, site of a Japanese air base. The Americans won the battle, but at a high cost. During the attack, Company E of the 28th Regiment of the Fifth Division reached the crest of Mount Suribachi (546 feet high), where several men raised the American flag. Joseph Rosenthal, a photographer accompanying the troops, memorialized this dramatic moment. (After the war, it was disclosed that the stirring photograph was a reenactment of the flag raising after the victory had been achieved.)

Sculptor Felix W. de Weldon was commissioned by the US Marine Corps in the early 1950s to honor the event by creating a bronze sculpture based on Rosenthal's photograph. The work is the largest sculpture ever cast in bronze; it weighs 100 tons, and each of the soldiers is almost 32 feet high. It was dedicated in 1954.

Tomb of the Unknown Soldier

This gigantic block of white Colorado marble stands at the approximate center of the cemetery. On November 11, 1921, the remains of an unknown American soldier of World War I were entombed here beneath the inscription: "Here rests in honored glory an American soldier known but to God." On Memorial Day 1958, an unknown soldier killed in World War II and another who died in the Korean conflict were interred in the marked crypts at the head of the tomb. Sentries stand guard here twenty-four hours a day; the guard is changed every half hour during the day and every two hours throughout the night.

GUNSTON HALL

10709 Gunston Road, Mason Neck. Open Thursday through Monday, 9:30 a.m. to 5 p.m. Closed Thanksgiving, December 25, and the first two weeks of January. General admission ranges from $1 to $12. Phone: (703) 550-9220.

This house was built from 1755 to 1758 by George Mason (1725–1792), a member of the Virginia House of Burgesses and author of the Virginia Declaration of Rights (1776). Although he was a framer of the United States Constitution (1787), he refused to sign the document because it contained weak tariff provisions and failed to abolish slavery.

Gunston Hall, Interior Room, Alexandria Area (LIBRARY OF CONGRESS, PRINTS AND PHO-TOGRAPHS DIVISION)

Four tall chimneys and a steep roof with dormers give this brick dwelling a dramatic appearance. The carved woodwork of the interior—the work of Englishman William Buckland—is among the finest found in this country. The Chinese Chippendale dining room he created here was the first of its kind in the colonies. Other impressive rooms are on display. The most important piece of furniture in the house is the writing table on which Mason drafted the Virginia Declaration of Rights. Mason's nine children received their early education in the schoolhouse near the mansion. The schoolmaster lived in the loft above the classroom.

The sprawling boxwood gardens overlooking the Potomac are in the English manor house tradition. Both Mason and his wife, Ann, are buried in the family cemetery on this estate.

WOODLAWN PLANTATION

9000 Richmond Highway, Alexandria. Open mid-April to mid-December, Thursday through Monday, 10 a.m. to 4 p.m. Guided tours at 10 a.m., 11 a.m., 1 p.m., 2 p.m., and 3 p.m. Adults $15, children (under 5) free, seniors $12, students $7.50. Phone: (703) 780-4000.

In 1799, George Washington gave a tract of his Mount Vernon estate as a wedding gift to Eleanor Parke Custis (Martha Washington's granddaughter) on her marriage to Major Lawrence Lewis (Washington's nephew). On this site the Lewises built an imposing Georgian mansion. It was designed by William Thornton, an intimate friend of the Washington family and a designer of the United States Capitol. While Woodlawn was being built, the young couple resided at Mount Vernon.

The Lewises' son Lorenzo inherited Woodlawn in 1839 and sold the estate in 1846. The property then passed through many hands until it was purchased in 1948 by the Woodlawn Public Foundation. In 1957, the title was transferred to the National Trust for Historic Preservation. The plan of this magnificent house—a wide central hallway with two rooms on either side—is typical of the period. The dining room, music room, parlor, and master bedroom are on the ground floor; the remaining bedrooms are located on the second floor.

Many of the furnishings here belonged to the Lewis family. Among the noteworthy pieces are a Hiram Powers bust of George Washington, a pianoforte, a Baltimore sideboard, Mrs. Lewis's four-poster bed, a painted Sheraton chair from Mount Vernon, and a marble-and-ormolu clock once owned by Lafayette (who visited this house in 1824). Examples of Mrs. Lewis's needlework are also on display.

The superb gardens were restored in the 1950s by the Garden Club of Virginia.

Mount Vernon

REVOLUTIONARY WAR HISTORY

Mount Vernon, George Washington's estate on the Potomac River, is perhaps America's most cherished historical shrine.

In 1669, John Washington (George Washington's great-grandfather) and Nicholas Spenser applied for a royal grant of 5,000 acres. Washington's share of the land they acquired eventually passed to his grandson Augustine (1726). In 1735, Augustine built a modest one-and-a-half-story house on this site and brought his wife and children from Wakefield. (George Washington was born at Wakefield in 1732.) When a fire destroyed the structure here in 1739, Augustine moved his family to an estate near Fredericksburg and gave this land to Lawrence, his oldest son (George's half brother).

George Washington by Gilbert Stuart (NATIONAL PORTRAIT GALLERY, SMITHSONIAN INSTITUTION; GIFT OF DONALD W. REYNOLDS FOUNDATION)

In 1743, Lawrence built a new house on this site, naming it "Mount Vernon" in honor of Admiral Edward Vernon, under whom he had served in the West Indies. When Lawrence died in 1752, the property passed to the twenty-year-old George Washington, who made it his permanent residence.

In January 1759, Washington brought his bride, Martha Dandridge Custis, a wealthy young widow, and her two children to live at Mount Vernon. The couple never had children of their own.

Wishing to enlarge the house, Washington made numerous architectural modifications: A second story was added (1758–1759), the length of the house was extended (1774, 1776), and a colonnaded porch was built (1780s). (During the Revolution a relative of Washington's managed the plantation and supervised the construction.) Washington increased the size of the estate from 2,126 acres to more than 8,000. Work on the plantation—which comprised farm land, orchards, workshops, mills, and distilleries—was done by several hundred slaves.

Washington died here in 1799 and was buried, as he had requested, on the estate grounds. When Martha died in 1802, Mount Vernon passed to George Washington's nephew, Bushrod Washington. After his death in 1829, the property passed through several hands until 1856, when it was purchased for $200,000 by the Mount Vernon Ladies Association. The association is responsible for the restoration and maintenance of the estate.

Mount Vernon completed a $40 million restoration from 2023 to 2025. The Reynolds Museum and Education Center, near the mansion, reopened in 2026 after extensive renovations.

MOUNT VERNON MANSION

3200 Mount Vernon Memorial Highway, Mount Vernon. Open daily April through October, 9 a.m. to 5 p.m.; November through March, 9 a.m. to 4 p.m. Purchase tickets at the Ford Orientation Center. Adults $30, youth (6–11) $16, children (under 5) free. Phone: (703) 780-2000.

Mount Vernon was George Washington's beloved home where he and Martha welcomed loyal friends, important statesmen, and military leaders.

Meticulous care has gone into every detail of the restoration—from copying original draperies and bed coverings to selecting appropriate examples of eighteenth-century furniture.

The distinctive feature of the **Banquet Hall,** the first room one enters, is the Palladian window. To the left of the window stands a

George Washington Receiving French Generals at Mount Vernon (detail), artist unknown (THE NATIONAL ARCHIVES, WASHINGTON, DC)

Hepplewhite sideboard, made in 1797 by John Aitken of Philadelphia. The marble mantel and the porcelain mantel vases were a gift of Washington's friend, Samuel Vaughan. Two engravings by John Trumbull, *The Death of General Montgomery* and *The Battle of Bunker's Hill*, adorn the walls.

In the **Central Hall**, several items original to the house are displayed: a spyglass, a barometer, a lantern, a clock, and a key to the Bastille (a gift from General Lafayette in 1790).

The **Little Parlor** contains the harpsichord that Washington imported from London in 1793 for his ward Nellie Custis. One of the engravings above the harpsichord depicts the 1779 naval battle between John Paul Jones's *Bonhomme Richard* and the British ship *Serapis*. The three oval mezzotints are of Washington, Franklin, and Lafayette.

The **West Parlor** is noted for its handsome mantelpiece, fine paneling, denticulated molding, and decorated ceiling. The gaming table, made in England in the 1750s, is the work of cabinetmaker Philip Bell. Among the painting reproductions are Charles Willson Peale's *George Washington*, James Sharple's *George Washington Lafayette* (Lafayette's son), and Robert Edge Pine's *Fanny Bassett* (Mrs. Washington's niece).

The elegant **Dining Room** is dominated by a Chippendale dining table on which is set a centerpiece—a mirrored plateau, which was a gift to Washington from Gouverneur Morris, a member of the Continental Congress and the Constitutional Convention. The ladder-back side chairs were made in Philadelphia in the early 1780s. The ornate mahogany Chippendale looking glass, with a scroll pediment and leaf motifs, belonged to Thomas Peter, who married Mrs. Washington's granddaughter, Martha Parke Custis. The Windsor high chair is said to have been used by children of the Custis family.

Five **Bedrooms** are located on the second floor. In **Washington's Bedroom** may be seen the portmanteau trunk acquired by the general in 1776 and used during the Revolutionary War. The shaving table and Mrs. Washington's desk are both French pieces, possibly purchased from the Comte de Moustier, the first minister of France to the United States. The two portraits, by Robert Edge Pine, are of Mrs. Washington's granddaughters.

The four-poster canopied bed is the one in which President Washington died on December 14, 1799. Two days earlier, while inspecting his lands, he was caught in a snowstorm and returned home wet and chilled. Despite the admonitions of his wife, he spent the evening attending to correspondence. The next day Washington treated the resulting cold and sore throat with household remedies. Suddenly his condition began to deteriorate; breathing became difficult, and pain racked his body.

On December 14, a servant was dispatched to Alexandria to bring the family physician, James Craik. Alarmed at the condition of his friend, Dr. Craik called in Dr. Gustavus Brown and Dr. Elisha Dick for consultation. The only treatment they could agree on, bloodletting, further weakened their sixty-seven-year-old patient. Sensing that death was near, Washington gave his final instructions to his secretary, Tobias Lear. Several hours later, at 10:02 p.m., Washington died.

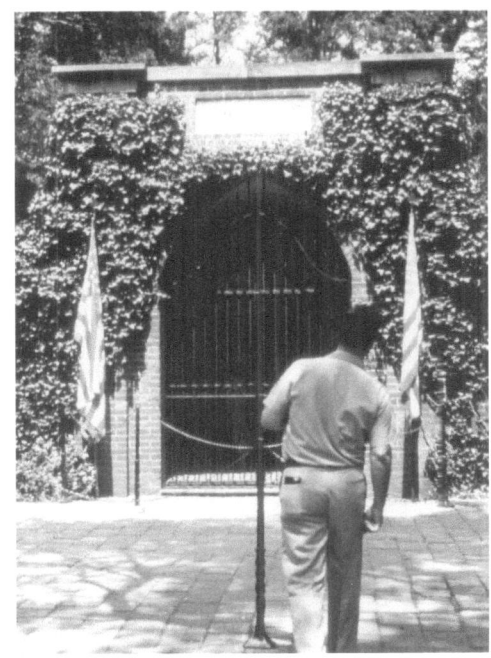

Washington's body was placed in a coffin bearing plates with the inscriptions "*Surge Ad Judicium*" (Rise for Judgment) and "*Glorio Deo*" (Thanks be to God). It was taken to the portico and set on a catafalque so that the crowds who had braved the bitter weather to come here could pay their respects.

Tomb of George Washington, Mount Vernon (ALPER)

On December 18, Washington was laid to rest in the family vault at Mount Vernon. As his coffin was carried by pallbearers to the vault, a military honor guard formed ranks at the gravesite, where the funeral service was performed. An artillery salute was fired from guns lining the river and from a warship anchored in the Potomac. As the sun was beginning to set, the heavy-hearted mourners turned homeward.

Thomas Jefferson spoke for the nation when he said of his fallen comrade, "His integrity was most pure, his justice the most inflexible I have ever known; no motives of interest, or consanguinity, or friendship, or hatred being able to bias his decision. He was indeed in every sense of the word, a wise, good and a great man."

INDEX

About the Author

Early in life, **Max Victor Alper** developed a passion for Colonial and Revolutionary War history. Several years ago he started traveling to Revolutionary War sites and to historical reenactments. He has served as a professor, writer, professional photographer, art gallery curator, and radio commentator.

He received his PhD from New York University, where he later served as a faculty member and administrator. He specialized in eighteenth-century literature, art, and history. As Director of Communication, Media and Arts, he was responsible for programs in art, photography, writing, and filmmaking.

Alper's fine art photographs have been shown in over 180 exhibitions in the United States and Europe. His work is included in private and public collections, including museums, and he has exhibited at numerous major galleries in New York City. Recently, his photographs were selected for exhibits at Art Basel Miami. In addition to numerous articles, reviews, and museum catalogs, Alper has written two books about American history and culture. Hundreds of photos were created for the project, and many appear in the books.

He has served on committees of several organizations, such as the National Endowment for the Humanities and the National Academy of Television Arts and Sciences (Emmy Division). Alper also has been an author/editor of *Arts Magazine* and has contributed art reviews and academic articles to national publications. He has written and narrated a radio series for WGBH-Boston and appeared on numerous radio and television programs. Alper has participated in the Fellows Program of the American Council on Education and has been awarded a residency at the prestigious American Academy in Rome, Italy.

He has worked at the Foley Gallery and other galleries in New York City. Currently, Alper divides his time between New York City and Pennsylvania.

Alper has written a companion book, *A Nation's Birth*, about the Revolutionary War and historic sites in the North.

www.ingramcontent.com/pod-product-compliance
Ingram Content Group UK Ltd.
Pitfield, Milton Keynes, MK11 3LW, UK
UKHW041837100626
6389IPUK00002B/37